"Their parents were told to expect nothing. But Jason Kingsley and Mitchell Levitz were lucky, because their parents didn't listen. They gave their sons that chance to show how far they could go—and they've astounded everyone! *Count Us In* tells their story—and asks the rest of us to throw out our outmoded notions about people with developmental disabilities."

**—Jane Pauley**

"I was struck by the poignant thoughts expressed by Kingsley and Levitz, and their connection to the basic precepts of the Americans with Disabilities Act—that disability is a natural part of the human experience and in no way diminishes the right of individuals with disabilities to live independently, enjoy self-determination, make choices, contribute to society, and experience full integration and inclusion into all aspects of society. This account illustrates inclusion, independence, and empowerment in action!"

**—Senator Tom Harkin**
**Chair, Subcommittee on Disability Policy**

# Count Us In

Growing Up with Down Syndrome

# Count Us In

## Growing Up
## with Down Syndrome

Jason Kingsley and Mitchell Levitz

*With a Foreword by* Joan Ganz Cooney

A Harvest Original

Harcourt Brace & Company

*San Diego    New York    London*

Library of Congress Catalog
Card Number: 93-27835

ISBN 0-15-150447-4
0-15-622660-X (pbk)

Designed by Lydia D'moch

Printed in the United States of America

First Harvest edition 1994
A B C D E

To protect the privacy of some of the people who appear
in this book, their names and certain details
about them have been changed.

To my mom and dad and Mitchell's mom and dad, two helpful families who made this all happen. I would like to thank my parents who made my whole life to the fullest.

**—Jason Kingsley**

Throughout my whole entire life and since I was born, my family has been there for me. This is why I feel that this book is important to me and to my family. At this time, I would like to dedicate this book to the people who I love the most, my family.

**—Mitchell Levitz**

# Contents

# Foreword

In the mid-1950s, when I was publicizing television shows in NBC's press department, I was asked to help with the advance publicity for a Roy Rogers–Dale Evans television special. In a package of background material I was given was a book by Dale Evans called *Angel Unaware*. It was the story of her and her family's experience with a daughter, born to her and Roy a few years earlier—a child who had Down syndrome. The little girl had died when she was only three years old.

Dale's book was an epiphany for me. Her description of her family's delight in that adorable and affectionate child moved me to tears. So did her account of their sense of loss and bereavement when their little girl died. Later Dale told me that one of her greatest satisfactions in the years after her book came out was seeing, at last, children with Down syndrome in the audiences that came to watch her and Roy perform.

By the early 1970s, I had long since left NBC and was deeply immersed in pioneering educational television for children. I had cofounded Children's Television Workshop and originated our flagship program for preschoolers, "Sesame Street," which began broadcasting in 1969. I had never completely forgotten Dale Evans and Roy Rogers's little angel, but I was reminded of her again personally and forcefully in 1974, when Emily Perl Kingsley, a writer for "Sesame Street," called from the hospital to tell me that her son, Jason, had been born with Down syndrome. Although he was only a few hours old, doctors were telling Emily and her husband, Charles, that Jason would never be capable of anything, physical or intellectual, and that he ought to be institutionalized. Even so, Emily and Charles were planning to bring Jason home and would try to bring him up themselves.

Remembering Dale Evans, I said something that probably sounded facile to Emily but with which I'm sure she would agree—something like, "It will be a very intense parenting experience." Emily will probably laugh out loud when she reads that quote.

In the months before Jason was born, we at "Sesame Street" had already begun discussing ways of including children with disabilities on the show. We had realized that if we were designing a series for preschoolers, we were talking about children of a certain developmental age as well as a chronological one. Since "Sesame Street" has always tried to include and reach as many children as possible, we knew we wanted to have kids with special learning needs on the show, and we had been discussing an adapted curriculum for them.

Thanks in part to Jason and Emily, "Sesame Street" soon began to include children with Down syndrome: when Jason was only fifteen months old, he made his television debut sitting on Buffy Sainte-Marie's lap. When he was six, we showed him counting in Spanish. Jason and Mitchell Levitz, who was three years older and also had Down syndrome, both appeared many times as two of the regular kids on the Street. In one show Mitchell, who enjoys playing soccer in real life, played soccer with Luis.

At first, we also did separate segments with a curriculum and activities for children with special learning needs. But we learned very quickly that these children didn't need a different format. So our next step was to demonstrate that they did not need to be segregated in special educational programs but could be part of a regular elementary school class. We showed Big Bird going to school for the first time. One of his classmates was Mitchell. The show opened our 1981 season, and we designed a poster showing Big Bird's class, with Mitchell in the front row.

I consider our decision to include these children as one of our finest achievements. I always will be grateful that Emily was among the earliest writers on the show and became a driving force behind the "Sesame Street" focus on children with special needs. Thanks to them, "Sesame Street" became the only show that routinely featured children with disabilities— without focusing on their disabilities.

Today, we can be proud of how much the world has changed since Dale Evans told me that children with Down syndrome were nearly always hidden from public view. Times have changed, thanks to parents like the Kingsleys and the Levitzes and to young people like Jason and Mitchell. Parents of other children with Down syndrome have told me how much it meant to them and their own kids to see Jason and Mitchell on "Sesame Street." And now we have events like the Special Olympics, television programs like "Life Goes On," and most important, new basic civil rights legislation.

The 1990 Americans with Disabilities Act prohibits discrimination against individuals with disabilities. It has often been described as the most sweeping nondiscrimination legislation since the Civil Rights Act of 1964. It provides broad-based nondiscrimination protection for individuals with disabilities in, among other areas, employment, public services, and public accommodations. Long overdue, this legislation will help greatly to make independent living for many more people with Down syndrome and other disabilities a reality instead of a dream.

Jason Kingsley and Mitchell Levitz make abundantly clear, to those who still may not know, what people with disabilities want. They want exactly what the rest of us want. The very fact that they have written *Count Us In* underscores that too many among us have greatly underestimated the potential skills and abilities of a sizable minority of the population. Jason and Mitchell are young heros for our time, and, thanks to them and their families and to others like them, the world faced by the new generation of children with Down syndrome is far more accepting than the one into which they were born.

And yet we as a society still have a long way to go. We are exceedingly careless in this country about wasting potential; we are persistently reluctant to invest in people at the front end of life in order to achieve a multiplicity of benefits in the long term. For example, we tend to forget that with enriched opportunities and high expectations many children with Down syndrome grow up to become responsible tax-paying citizens who contribute to their communities in many ways. Jason, now a senior in high school, is looking into higher education and career opportunities, while Mitchell is working and paying taxes and has just moved into his own house. We cannot relearn too often the great lesson of "Sesame Street": if you work with any child who is disadvantaged—physically, intellectually, or socioeconomically—he or she will do better, sometimes amazingly better.

Jason has said, "Give a baby with a disability a chance to grow a full life. To experience a half-full glass instead of the half-empty glass. And think of your abilities, not your disabilities."

Can we do less than he suggests? I think not.

— *Joan Ganz Cooney*

# Introduction

by Emily Perl Kingsley
and Barbara Gibbs Levitz

**Barbara:** Absolutely nothing prepares you for being told that your newborn child is "less than perfect." Mitchell was born April 10, 1971, and for the next few days things just didn't seem *right*. The baby never seemed to cry. He was having trouble feeding and wasn't opening his eyes. The nurses seemed to be avoiding me, and I began to feel nervous about what was going on. The excitement and joy of having my first child were dampened by the confusion and by the mixed messages I was receiving. I finally demanded to know what was going on. The doctor responded by telling me that he planned to run some tests, but he never shared with me what he suspected.

That's when I started to look to my background as a special education teacher and to draw my own conclusions. I finally asked the doctor if he was testing for Down syndrome. When he answered yes, I wanted to share my feelings of disappointment and sadness with my husband, Jack. But if the tests proved negative, then I could spare Jack that pain. So, as I quietly scrutinized my baby's tiny features, I struggled to keep all those feelings inside for almost a week until I received the confirmation.

And then our lives changed forever.

I should explain that from the time I was in high school, and worked with children who had Down syndrome in a summer camp, I had determined to pursue a career teaching children with special needs. I had learned in college that Down syndrome is a genetic disorder caused by the presence of an extra chromosome; it is rarely ever hereditary. I knew that children with Down syndrome experience delays in their development and often certain medical problems as well. But I had also learned from my experience as a special education teacher that each has his or her own individual personality and range of abilities.

However, in spite of all of that knowledge, and years of training, involvement, and experience, nothing prepared me for this. It's completely different when this happens to your own baby and your own family. Our devastation was compounded when the doctor told us that our son's mental retardation would be a burden to us and recommended that the baby be institutionalized.

We knew that this was not what we wanted for our son. Two issues most concerned us. First, we wanted to find a way to help Mitchell learn and grow and live the fullest life possible. Second, we were angry at the way this situation had been handled and were determined to do whatever we could to lessen the nightmare for other families in the same position.

That was the beginning of the fight—and the beginning of the Parent Assistance Committee on Down Syndrome. We started by reaching out to other families who felt the same way we did. I searched the files of children with Down syndrome whom I had taught locally, and contacted their families. And they in turn found other families. We all shared the same traumatic early experience and the same goals: to make it easier for other families, to learn more ourselves, to get programs and services for our children, and to try to improve the public's understanding of Down syndrome.

By this time, Mitchell was about a year old and we were delighted with his development and the unexpected happiness he brought to our lives. We enrolled him in a new and experimental type of program, called Early Intervention, which provided physical therapy to help improve his development. Over the next few years, he was able to begin attending our community nursery school and was turning out to be an adorable, mischievous, bright little boy.

**Emily:** Jason was born on June 27, 1974, and was diagnosed as having Down syndrome when he was only a few hours old. Like many other parents, my husband, Charles, and I were told by the doctor, "Your child will be mentally retarded. He'll never sit or stand, walk or talk. He'll never be able to distinguish you from any other adults. He'll never read or write or have a single meaningful thought or idea. The common practice for these children is to place them in an institution immediately." This doctor went so far as to say, "Go home and tell your friends and family that he died in childbirth."

Other professionals we consulted reinforced this philosophy. One psychologist suggested that raising a child like this would put extreme pressure and strain on our marriage and that the constant disappointment over the years would surely destroy our family.

After several days of crying, and soul searching, and reading what little information was available at that time (most of which was depressing and frightening), Charles and I made the difficult decision to disregard the professional advice and bring Jason home. It didn't make sense to us to send our newborn child away without giving him a few days, a few weeks of our time, to see from our own experience what he was like.

Charles's two teenage sons, Glenn and Todd, were wonderfully supportive. "Of course you're going to bring him home," they exclaimed. "He's our brother!" But in truth, none of us knew exactly what was in store for our family.

The first few months were an agony of loneliness. There was no one to talk to who could really understand exactly how we felt or share the pain, the disappointment, and the fear.

Then one day I opened the local newspaper and spotted an ad that read: "Parents of children with Down syndrome will meet at the Prudential Bank Monday at 8:00 P.M." There were others! Other parents, other people sharing the same experiences and feelings!

Charles and I eagerly attended the meeting and were astonished and overjoyed to find a room full of people who were actually laughing, conversing, and proudly exchanging photographs of their adorable children!

It was the Parent Assistance Committee on Down Syndrome, established by Barbara and Jack Levitz three years earlier after Mitchell was born. The Levitzes had been given much of the same information and advice and the same gloomy prognosis for Mitchell. Yet at age three, Mitchell was a delightful bundle of energy, nothing like what the doctors had predicted.

That meeting with the Levitz family represented the beginning of many things: a warm, close relationship between our two families that has endured and grown over the past nineteen years, a partnership of energy and commitment to helping other people and changing public attitudes about children like ours, and a lifelong friendship between Jason and Mitchell.

In a sense, it also was the beginning of this book.

**Emily and Barbara:** For nearly two decades, our families have shared our joys and problems, the emotional roller coaster of soaring successes and plummeting disappointments, daily frustrations and challenges, and exciting accomplishments and achievements.

We've supported one another and shared strategies for dealing with recalcitrant school districts, obstinate camp directors, misinformed and insensitive children and adults who occasionally made rude remarks or hurt our children's feelings.

We've also shared the thrill of seeing the boys continually overcome and surpass the limited expectations that others had for them. And, most important, we've shared the joy of discovering that they were developing into two very caring, imaginative, hardworking, generous, spunky, self-motivated, and interesting boys.

In looking back, we've learned that what was most important was *not* their level of intellectual achievement, but rather their personal qualities of warmth and sincerity and their contributions to their family, friends, and acquaintances. In addition, we have learned the folly of attempting to predict a person's quality of life based on his or her label or condition. These boys have succeeded because they were given opportunities and allowed to take risks, and because we refused to let anyone write them off.

**Emily:** The friendship between our families has been especially helpful to Charles and me, since Mitchell is three years older than Jason. We could always turn to Barbara and Jack for information and reinforcement as a result of their additional experience. Whenever Charles and I were concerned about a particularly troublesome phase, Barbara would calmly reassure us, "Oh don't worry. We had exactly the same thing with Mitchell at that age. Jason will grow out of it."

**Barbara:** Similarly, whenever Jack and I were feeling discouraged and frustrated, tired of constantly having to open new doors, break new ground, and create new opportunities, Emily and Charles were there for moral support and encouragement.

**Emily and Barbara:** Over the years, we have struggled against the prevailing philosophy that children with Down syndrome were, by definition, not educable. Many school districts believed it was inappropriate to include children with Down syndrome in regular schools or regular classes and that it was a waste of time to attempt to teach them academics. This was unacceptable to us because we had already observed that the boys were capable of more, so we urged educators to allow the boys opportunities that were commensurate with their abilities.

There were battles, struggles, defeats, and much hard work. Our attitude was "Just give it a try and see if it works; if not, we'll understand and try something different." We were fortunate to encounter some more progressive teachers and school administrators who were willing to try an experimental approach. Ultimately Mitchell and Jason themselves were able to prove that they could handle educational and social challenges that had previously been thought impossible for them.

Fortunately, Jason and Mitchell thrived in public school. In an environment of encouragement and optimism they constantly surprised and delighted us — and their teachers — with accomplishments we'd never dreamed of. With the ever-growing love and support of other family members and friends, their lives were further enriched by a tremendous sense of belonging and security. And as their confidence and abilities increased, one success built on another.

It became more and more apparent that the early predictions had terribly underestimated the boys' capabilities, and our two families became increasingly committed to dispelling the old misconceptions and to sending out a more hopeful message about the potential of children like Mitchell and Jason. We accompanied the boys to speak at scores of medical schools, nursing programs, professional organizations, community groups, and elementary and secondary school classes. There were exciting television and radio interviews. Articles appeared in newspapers and magazines. Seizing any and all opportunities to enhance the public's awareness and understanding of Down syndrome became part of our daily lives.

We are encouraged that babies with Down syndrome nowadays will benefit from a more enlightened attitude about their entitlement to full participation in all aspects of community life. What was for us a continual confrontation is now beginning to be accepted as sound educational practice and, in fact, the right of all children.

Today, youngsters with disabilities are attending school and recreation programs together with their peers without disabilities. Parents will be spared the constant sadness and frustration that results from segregating and devaluing children with special needs. As children grow up together and learn to understand and appreciate each other, this integration will simply become a natural part of life. This is especially important when we consider that these children will be the doctors, teachers, community members, friends, *and parents* of tomorow.

When Mitchell and Jason entered adolescence, we faced new challenges. As is typical with teenagers, we found the boys engaging in a tremendous amount of self-examination, intense focus on relationships, and reflection on their identity. This involved much exploration of self-esteem issues and grew into a deep analysis of their own disability. Their increasing self-awareness itself was contrary to the early beliefs: that young people like Jason and Mitchell would never be bright enough to conceptualize the fact that they had a disability. But they *were* able to conceptualize it, and they had their own need to discuss it and begin to work through it.

And we were impressed with many things: the depth of their insights and perceptions, the breadth of their knowledge, their reactions to the world and excitement about their experiences, the intensity of their belief in themselves and their rights to full participation, their dignity and integrity as human beings, and the immense scope and richness of their dreams.

Mitchell and Jason had *a lot* to talk about, and it seemed deeply important to them to do so. We felt it might also be valuable for them to share some of their insights with other young people with and without Down syndrome.

**Emily:** In the summer of 1990, Barbara said, "How about a book?" Immediately the idea seemed right. The boys were enthusiastic and couldn't wait to begin.

Mitchell was a junior in high school, and Jason was in the eighth grade, preparing to enter high school. The two boys, Barbara, and I would cluster around the Macintosh computer in my office at home. During our early sessions, Barbara and I would get the ball rolling by suggesting a topic for discussion. As the boys spoke, I would type as fast as I could and take down everything that was said. Fortunately, Jason and Mitchell speak a little more slowly than people who don't have Down syndrome, so it was possible for me to get everything down without hampering the spontaneity and enthusiasm of the conversation.

On a few occasions, we attempted to tape-record the discussions and later transcribe them for the book. However, because of the boys' mild speech articulation and fluency problems, we found that taping and transcribing the conversations was less effective than typing their statements directly into the computer.

**Emily and Barbara:** We collected over fifty transcripts of Mitchell and Jason's conversations. In addition to the regular sessions, the boys also had some special talks with their fathers, their grandfathers, and their friends. They also made some individual written contributions.

Over the course of the three years spent working on this book, we became less and less involved in the process as the boys gained confidence and trust in each other and in their ability to express and share their thoughts. Mitchell and Jason also grew in their commitment to the "mission" of the book: to educate and enlighten people about what it's like to be a teenager today and what it's like to have Down syndrome.

They started suggesting their own topics for discussion and, in the process, real dialogue emerged. They asked each other's advice on complicated issues of growing up and inde-

pendence. They helped each other work through difficult situations and offered mutual support and reassurance.

Because of their three-year age difference, they have always
been at different stages of development. But as we watched
Mitchell and Jason grow and mature, it became apparent that
they are two very separate and unique individuals. They have
their own distinct preferences, interests, and areas of expertise.
They have their own styles and personalities. At the same time,
they share a tremendous mutual respect and affection, which
grew even deeper as a result of their collaboration on this project. It was beautiful to witness.

So here it is.

This book is in Mitchell and Jason's own words. While the
material has been pared down somewhat,* no attempt has
been made to "correct" their sometimes idiosyncratic syntax or
expression. The boys have a developmental disability, after all,
and we have no desire to hide or camouflage that fact. Rather,
we wanted readers to have a true-to-life sense of their charm,
their directness, their humor and warmth, and, yes, their intelligence. We are immensely proud of our sons, and we hope
that you will find their book to be as moving, as poignant, and,
occasionally, as profound as we have in the course of its
creation.

---

*Cuts in Mitchell and Jason's passages are indicated throughout by the use of ellipses
and line spaces.

# 1
# About This Book

## "Every Single One Counts"

**Jason:** I hope a lot of people will read this book. They will learn that people with Down syndrome can share the same feelings as disabled and nondisabled kids.

And in the time line of history, in 1993 it will say: "Jason and Mitchell wrote a book!"

*March '91*

**Jason:** But there's a problem about this book here. That some people may not read this book.

**Emily:** Yes, I certainly wish that everybody would read this book!

**Jason:** You mean to tell me that the Persian Gulf guys, that Saddam Hussein should read this book?

**Emily:** I think it would be nice if *everybody* in the whole world would read this book—but I don't think that's too realistic. I doubt that Saddam Hussein will ever read this book. But that's okay. If a lot of people here in the United States read it, that will make me very happy.

**Jason:** And the president? And the news?

**Emily:** That would be nice.

**Jason:** People would understand more about people like me with Down syndrome who have this problem. I really wish Down syndrome would be on the news. They could tell us news about Down syndrome on television. Like: "And now the news! A Down syndrome is someone who was born with an extra chromosome. A Down syndrome kid can be special in the normal outside world with everybody else. They can live in a regular house and work in a regular school and work in a regular job. 'Cause they're just like everybody else — except different because they have Down syndrome. That's very different because when you have Down syndrome your learning might be slow. That's your disability. Sometimes it's a big disability that they have."

The commercials. The commercials should know about Down syndrome, too. People with Down syndrome and sometimes people without Down syndrome should be in the commercials. And they will read: "The best part of waking up is Down syndrome Folgers in your cup!" "We're all connected — Down syndrome Telephone!" "Buckle up with Down syndrome — it's the law!" "Get Down syndrome — it's the real thing!" "Get Down syndrome — don't leave home without it!"

**Mitchell:** I think I have a perfect title for this book. I think we should name this book *The Successful Story of Having Down Syndrome*.

*May '92*

**Mitchell:** I want all people to read this book so they can understand the perspectives of two young adults who have Down syndrome . . . so that they can understand the same situations that we were involved in.

**Jason:** I think this book can accomplish by teaching how people with disabilities and people not with disabilities can learn more and be more understanding about us because we also are a part of life. They will understand how it is to be ourselves and how it is to be themselves. To feel a part of this whole life . . .

They can change their views when they're thinking about people with disabilities and with Down syndrome. They thought before that we never can be understanding, and they are insulting us that we are not smart than anyone else. Now when they read this book they'll change and they'll think about the good parts of life can lead us into a good happy life.

There are parts of life that you have to deal with. Social life: You have to associate with others like go to parties together, hang around. Lovelife: like you and your girlfriend. Family life is having your family and independence. And fun life is to be joyful and playful. All that is lead up to a big world of *life*.

And another part of life is your disabled life. Your disabled life is what you see in yourself, what you're accomplishing even though you have a disability and pain. What you're accomplishing by doing the best you could.

**Mitchell:** And living independently is another part of the success. By living independently away from your parents is important so you could realize the important part of the other life. The other life is living on your own and taking responsibility for yourself. By taking responsibilities for yourself is a new meaning of life to the next stage. You're taking your life farther. Toward the future.

And my future, not only to live independently... for my future is to live my life the way I want to be instead of being told how I should live my life, either by my parents or by the people I live with. They are not the ones to tell me how should I run my life. Because I feel it is my decision to make. Nobody else's. Because that's another part of the success, by dictating to people the way you want your life. By taking the initiative and the responsibilities yourself instead of people telling you this is your life, this is the way you have to live it. It's not.

Part of life is you deal with situations yourself. Because we put ourself in situations, we have to take ourselves out of situations. Even with the support of family and community and loved ones as well.

**Jason:** And making decisions is part of your own life, too. Decisions of your disabled life. That means you're deciding the things you're trying to accomplish and doing the best you could.

I could change my disabled life with Down syndrome by doing the best that I can do and to teach people how they would understand because it might be difficult with a disability because you may be very slow.

Down syndrome is a part of your disabled life. Even though you have the pain and you want the pain stopped, you still have it. All you have to do is lift up your anxieties and do all the good parts of your life.... All you have to do is live with it. Even though you have the pain, but work things out to make it a good one.

I realize from there [that] I really want to have Down syndrome because I would be missing some good things about my disabled life ... about special ed, your parents, how does it affect your girlfriend, your lovelife, and now you want to have this disability. Because you can keep doing a lot of stuff and enjoy the good things to have some fun in your life. Be passionate of your life. Even if you have Down syndrome.

**Mitchell:** If I cannot change my disability, I would deal with it in any case because I know for sure that nobody can change their disability. It will be a difficult process to do so.

I was born with Down syndrome, and I said to my parents that I have overcome my disability. I believe that I've come so far and that's been very successful. I believe that I did overcome, by being successful, having Down syndrome.

I believe that even though I've succeeded in my life, that I can change my life the way I see to it. In some senses it really doesn't have any more challenges left for me because I feel that I can take any risks or anything that comes to me in any way.... I can face those tasks with some help, but I can do the most part by myself.

**Jason:** I didn't overcome it. Because there's some things that I still have to learn that my parents can teach me things. But somehow when I get older I can overcome my disability, but right now I have to adjust to it.

I have to do the easy parts and the good parts of this whole life. I'm doing as much as I can, but I still have a way to go but my disability never changes. I have to change my life and somehow my disability automatically can overcome. Somehow, somewhen...my disability can overcome.

*December '92*

**Mitchell:** The important thing about having a disability [is] that you should think about this disability and it can encourage you a lot. It's an encouragement knowing who you are.

You're an individual, an adult with disability, who can handle any issue, tackle any issue. It's part of being an adult, knowing who you are, understanding who you are. Because we are people who understand, knowing about our disability.

People can change, people can realize you are an individual and an identity is important to you, to your family, even to your community. People consider you an individual with rights. People respect you for who you are. Not just your disability. The person who you are makes it. That's what counts. That's why we call this book *Count Us In*. We are individuals and they are counting us in.

**Jason:** After people read this book, strangers will become our friends.

**Mitchell:** *Count Us In* means that everyone together are helping each other out...by reaching out, by helping each other, which what it means is we want to be included. *Count Us In* makes the future better for people with disabilities.

Every single one counts because we are an important asset in the community and they need our voice.

# 2

# Who We Are

## "People Like Me for My Charm"

*Fall '90*

*The following is excerpted from a piece Mitchell wrote for a class assignment. He has added a few additional comments.*

On April 10th 1971, the birth of Mitchell Andrew Levitz was at the Peekskill Community Hospital and the parents of the child were Barbara and Jack Levitz. The Doctor told Barbara and Jack that the child had Down syndrome. This changed how they lived. My mother was one of the founders of the Parent Assistance Committee on Down Syndrome and I was one of the first children in Westchester in an Early Intervention Program.

I grew up and lived my entire life in the Peekskill Cortlandt Manor area in Westchester. Both of my parents also grew up here. Most of my family also live in Peekskill/Cortlandt Manor and had held businesses in this area.

Stephanie was born in 1972 and Leah in 1974 and they are both of my sisters. I attended First Hebrew Congregation of Peekskill Nursery School and Hebrew School with Stephanie. I went to a pre-primary class with Cantor Dennis Waldman who was also the Cantor for my Bar Mitzvah.

I attended kindergarten at Our Montessori School for one year and then Woodside Elementary School for two years in a

BOCES [Board of Cooperative Educational Services] Special Education Communications Class. After that I went to my local schools in Special Education classes for students with learning disabilities and some mainstream classes also. I went to Lincoln Titus Elementary School up to fifth grade, and I was in cub scouts and Weblos scouts. I got an Arrow of Light award and played soccer with AYSO [American Youth Soccer Organization] on weekends and got a lot of trophies and made friends.

I went to Lakeland Middle School for sixth grade. I skipped seventh grade and went into eighth grade. In middle school I had many teachers for different classes who helped me with many subjects. Some of the courses I took were math, history and sciences, chorus and art, phys. ed. and also speech therapy. I was in a traveling soccer league and played in a tournament at West Point.

When I was fourteen, I got working papers on my birthday to be able to work as a busboy at Colonial Terrace, my family's business, with Aunt Sheila and Uncle Alan and my father Jack. I liked working the parties with the other students from my school that the managers hired, and we became friends by working together. I worked there on weekends all through high school.

I have been at Walter Panas High School since ninth grade. I have took most of the required courses and exams and only have the reading exam left to pass to get a regular diploma. I also have to pass English, phys. ed. and politics/economics, and I am taking theater this year. I am on the Legislative Action Committee for the Board of Education and attend meetings. In Walter Panas I also took mainstream typing and computers, business ownership and management, and work experience in school in the Dean's office and out of school as a volunteer intern in a legislative office. I also played soccer my second years in high school and got a varsity letter.

My two sisters and I went to Camp Mill Run, a day camp,

for many years, that my Aunt Fran and Uncle Ed used to own. It was interesting and fun. The other camps I went to were Camp White Oaks, a sleep-away camp...[and] Camp Ramah, a sleep-away camp in Massachusetts.

...When I was young with both my sisters and my parents and sometimes other people in the family like Barry, Leon, and Annie and sometimes friends, we went camping in the summertime. When we go camping, we went hiking, rowing boats, fishing, swimming, and we also sing songs by the campfire and tell ghost stories and roast marshmallows and take pictures of the scenery and ourselves.

At one time in my life, I felt that I had a memorable moment that was important in my life. It was my Bar Mitzvah.... Rabbi Josh Hammerman helped me and my two sisters to go through a time of studying and preparation for Bar and Bat Mitzvahs, and was always there to turn to.... I learned then to be thirteen is to be between two worlds, the past of childhood and the promise of adulthood. My mother wrote a song to me on my Bar Mitzvah...called "The Best of Me." It meant a lot to me....

People make me feel important in life, especially my family with all of their love and support. I got guidance from my parents being there when I needed them, plus my sisters were the same way.... Stephanie and Leah have been very helpful, very supportive to me, who gave me a lot of potential. They have shown me what is right and wrong and also let me know how supportive I have been to them.

Some important events happened in my life. I went to a march in New York City for Soviet Jews. I also met Governor Mario Cuomo and his wife at a dinner for the Special Olympics. What they did for the disabled was a wonderful feeling to me. Recently I went to Albany and Assemblyman George Pataki said to the whole entire Assembly and to the speaker,

I would appreciate it if you could welcome to the chamber this afternoon an extraordinary young man from my district. He was born with Down syndrome and often that is something that results in that child being placed away from the mainstream and not involved academically and socially in the usual activities of childhood. And through the extraordinary efforts of his mother and father, Barbara and Jack Levitz, and through his own extraordinary efforts, he has led an exemplary life. He is now a junior at Walter Panas High School in the Town of Cortlandt, working as an intern in my district, coming in and helping me with constituent programs. We expect to see him graduate from high school next year and go on to lead a successful life and run against one of us some year. I wish you would recognize his courage and dedication. Seated behind me, Mitchell Levitz. [*Applause and standing ovation*]

I felt very warmed and honored. This was another special moment in my life. I am very interested in politics and government.

I was also on television. I was on the "NBC Weekend Show" and "The Morning Show with Regis and Kathie Lee," and on "Sesame Street" for two years. Since I was young, my family and I were in some articles in newspapers such as the *New York Times, USA Today,* Gannett, and some magazines also.... One was about the show "Life Goes On" starring Chris Burke who I've known for many years, and I enjoy watching the show a lot. I spoke to one of the writers to help out with a story for the show....

I spoke at a parent/professional conference as a keynote speaker along with Senator Nick Spano. Generally I enjoy talking to groups of people. I wasn't nervous when I gave a keynote speech along with Senator Libous for the New York State ARC [Association for Retarded Children] Convention for six hundred people in November [1991], and a speech for the New York State Self-Advocacy Association in September [1991]. My pictures have been in pamphlets, magazines, newspapers, and in a health book. I spoke to many health classes about having Down syndrome.

I have traveled a lot, with a group of young adults who have disabilities, during the summer with Summit Travel.... I already have gone to California, Hawaii, Canada, and this summer to Colorado with the group. During the rest of the year, they organize City Lights, where we meet our friends in New York City and we go to plays, restaurants, ball games, and a cruise around the city. I also traveled with my family. We went to Israel, Spain, and to Puerto Rico. We always have fun on these trips together.

There are people who I care about and are important to me in my life. These friends are supportive and understanding. One of my friends is the Dean of Students for Walter Panas High School, Mort David. He was there to help me understand the regulations of the school and help me with my problems I had with other students. He made me realize that school is important and to take my classes seriously.

Tom Fedge who lives in Cape Cod is also important to me. When I go to the Cape, I have a fun time. Tom wanted me to ride a bike.... I tried it out and it was fun. We would also take walks to the beach and talk about events in the world. My father...and Tom were roommates at Syracuse University. He and his family...are good friends to me and my family. They come to visit every New Year's and other times. We go places together.

My grandfather George Gibbs has contributed a lot to me. He would help me study and prepare for tests in my classes, and to remember what he helped me learn. We would also go out to lunch and go shopping together.... He also gives me advice on how I should make good decisions that will affect my life in the future.

Bob Brown, who lives in Washington, D.C., is my friend. He would tell me what is going on in Washington and discuss sports.

Seth Greenberg and I have lots of things in common, like wrestling and sports. When I go over to his house, we play Nintendo...and we challenge our fathers to play Ping-Pong. Harry Greenberg is Seth's father. He and myself have been close friends. He also helped me out why I had problems with people.... I call him not only as a friend because he is like a lawyer to me and he draws up legal papers or tells me how to handle situations from a legal standpoint.

Jason Kingsley also has Down syndrome. He appeared on television shows himself. Jason and I are friends and we get together and play games and talk about school. He is fun to do things with and he is also funny with the jokes he makes. The magic he does is fascinating.

I have a strong interest in politics, government and world affairs. I enjoy listening to music, watching wrestling and basketball on television, hanging out with friends, reading the newspaper every day, downhill skiing and water skiing, Ping-Pong and tennis.

I have a great personality and people like me for my charm. I like my personality and I have lots of friends who care and understand me well. Part of my personality is that I find women attractive and I like to flirt with them and use sexy words to get them interested in me. I care and understand about other people around me. Another part of my personality is that people take advantage of me because I am giving.

Now I am a senior at Walter Panas High School and I am going to graduate in June of 1991 with a regular diploma. After Panas, I am planning to go to a vocational program in South Orange, New Jersey.... I am going to be placed on a waiting list. This place I am planning to go to is called Jespy House.

In the future, I would like to work for the government or to manage my own business. That means to hire my own workers and to use my mind and to be creative in the work I will do in the future when I grow up. Someday I would like to be President of the United States.

*Spring '92*

*The following is excerpted from a piece Jason wrote for a class assignment.*

I was born on June 27, 1974, 11:04 P.M. in New York Hospital. I saw my loving parents Charles and Emily Kingsley. My father is a contractor in a painting company called J. M. Charles Painting Company. My mother is an author of "Sesame Street."

I have a disability called Down syndrome. My bad obstetrician said that I would never learn and send me into a institution and never see me again. No way Jose! Mom and Dad brought me home and taught me things.

We lived in 161 Finmor Drive in White Plains. I saw my brothers Glenn and Todd.... They had a different mother from my mom but they have the same dad. Todd is the tallest but Glenn is the oldest.... Glenn is eighteen years old and Todd is fifteen years old when I was born. I have a dog named Juneau.

When I was ten days old I went to M.R.I. [Mental Retardation Institute] with Dr. Giannini.... She said I would learn, slowly but a lot and I would be great. I started Infant Stimulation.... My Mom had put me in Jello, it was yummy and also put me into Styrofoam, it was yucky. This was to stimulate my senses. This stimulation also taught me to walk and talk. When I was one year old I had my first birthday.

At two years old I went to WARC [Westchester Association for Retarded Citizens] Preschool in White Plains. I stayed there for two years. I was two to four in that time. I learned letters, counted numbers, read a lot, and songs.... I went on "Sesame Street," it was great. I had fun. I went in[to] Oscar's trash can.

At age four to five I went to Alcott Montessori School. In that I learned to read. My first word was sock and doc. I started to give talks with a lot of people. We do that because we have to show them that I can learn.

When I was five years old I went to "All My Children." I acted myself on there.... I was supposed to be a little boy with Down syndrome. My Mom went on with me. At age seven I went on the show called "A. M. Philadelphia" in Pennsylvania. It was a talk show.... I counted in twelve foreign languages and sign languages.

Then my Mom was thinking to put me into a high academic Lakeland program in a different school out of district. So I went to Lakeland schools, Ben Franklin.... We saw an incubator from the farm with some eggs and we waited until the twenty-first day the eggs will hatch into chicks. And also I did some of those routine day jobs.... Each day I had to do a different job, like I am responsible to carry the juice at snack time. Somebody else did the blackboard, sweeping the floors.... Now it is my turn to do the dishes.

At age eight both my brothers got married with my sisters-in-law.... It was fancy. I wore a tuxedo.

At age ten I acted in "The Fall Guy" in 1984. We went to Hollywood to 20th Century Fox studios.... I acted with Lee Majors, the stunt man; Doug Barr, Lee's friend; Larry Holmes, the famous boxer; Bruce Jenner, the worker for Special Olympics; Lou Ferrigno, the Incredible Hulk; and Evan Richards, [who played] my brother.

My contribution to "The Fall Guy" was for me to memorize a sixty-four page script. It was two weeks to film. I had my own trailer for resting and my academic work. My academic work was from my teachers back from New York gave to me to do when I am relaxing.

I loved working to Lee Majors. He was my friend. In the show he was a stranger. The main idea of "The Fall Guy" was a stunt man helped a little kid at Christmas time to get to Special Olympics and solve the murder. Those two murderers said that

I don't know what I saw. But I did and I helped by escaping to get to Special Olympics on time.

When I came home from Hollywood I did not expect a letter from Chris Burke. It was a fan letter. I didn't even know Chris Burke then. He saw my "Fall Guy" show.... He wanted to be an actor too. I was the inspiration for him. I helped him be a part of one pilot series for "Life Goes On." Now he is a big star because I helped him. He is still my friend. Now he is twenty-six years old. When he comes to New York we go out to dinner together.

And speaking of dinners, we went to a Guest of Honor dinner with the Governor in New York State, Mario Cuomo. [While] Mr. Cuomo was busy finding his speech...there was an emcee saying, "And now ladies and gentlemen, the Mayor of Vaudevallette [Watervliet]." And Mr. Cuomo was still looking at his speech. I looked at him and said to him, "Clap!" and Governor broke up...and then clapped and then I said that was better.

In school they put me in a program called Special Ed with disabled kids. It was okay but it was far away from home. It was forty-five minutes on the bus, seventeen miles. But I learned a lot, slowly in a long period of time.

In the summers I went to day camps which was camp during the day and then I went back home after swimming. That's so I could exercise my physical body.

Tami is my girlfriend who was one year behind me in age. At the convention I saw Tami. She also has Down syndrome. That was the National Down Syndrome Congress in Cincinnati. And I had my first kiss and my first love letter from Tami. And we had workshops at conventions with her. The workshops were Sex Education, Future Life Planning, Job Skills, Grooming Nice. And Safety Tips when my parents wasn't around, when I'm alone.

My middle years I went to Copper Beech Middle School. Middle school was difficult. I did some academic stuff [and] my teachers had me read the Life Skills book. Life Skills Math — counting money, add money, subtracting, comparing.

In middle school people teased me because they think that is fun. They said words to me that I don't like. They called me names. I'm not comfortable when people tease me and my teachers sat with my parents and said this program doesn't pertain to me. So they put me into a Departmentalized Program which is more challenging. And things improved. They were nicer to me. But not too much. When it's time to do my Science test, some of the Departmentalized people did make noise during the test so I couldn't concentrate.... But I did okay....

During this period we were doing a CBS show called "Kids Like These." It was a movie about showing the people how well a disabled boy can learn. My mom and her friend Allan Sloane had wrote it. It was a takeoff on our life of our family.

I watched them filmed it. I get to know five kids who played me when I was younger. Tyne Daly was in it and Richard Crenna.... And Tyne Daly's father was Martin Balsam.

My relationship with Tyne Daly was good because we liked her and she was my mother in spirit. My mother in spirit means that she played my mother in the movie.

During middle years I went to Camp Lee-Mar. I met some friends there.... It was a nice camp. I was a camper-worker. The first job I did was sorting out the mail. The second job I did was sorting out the silverware. And my third job was teaching little kids. I taught them how to use a computer, how to use a pencil, then teach them how to write postcards every Sunday.

During my Middle Years I also practiced the piano with Shelley Robbins. She was a good teacher. I played kid songs and Mozart and Bach. That was a time that I knew the composers by then—Bach, Brahms, Tchaikovsky, Beethoven, Mozart.

And I started to love Broadway musicals.... I practically know all Broadway shows and all the Broadway songs. I listen to them in the car and we play games with it. I love to sing along.

In my later years, I went to Lakeland High School.... I've been in the Honor Roll since that I was in high school. My work is not easy and not hard but I did very well. I am doing my RCTs [Regents Competency Tests]. I passed two of them [so far]—Science and Math.

Now I am studying for my other RCT which is called History—Global Studies—for two years of high school world history. I am studying all my cultures in ninth and tenth grade, which are: Africa, Latin America, South and Southeast Asia, Afghanistan, Lebanon, Israel and the Middle East and Eastern Europe. Also the cultures I didn't cover yet like China, Japan, and Russia and Western Europe....

And now I am coming up to eighteen. Let me tell you what my future goal of being eighteen is. Being eighteen I have to be eligible to vote. This is a Presidential Election. I am voting for my President. Who? Clinton? vs. Bush. Or Ross Perot. I haven't decided who I'm going to vote for. I have to listen to the campaign.

Now I am older enough for me to decide things for myself alone. I can make my right decisions and that's the big part of independence. With no one helping me and I think I got potential to do it.

And being eighteen also in school I may be interested in only one girl, that's close to my life. Tami is fine. She is my girlfriend in Pittsburgh far away. I wish I had a girlfriend close and part of it is a girlfriend in school. Because I see a lot of boyfriends having good girlfriends in school already and I am the only one without a girl in school. It's very hard to find a girl who doesn't have a boyfriend.

During the tenth grade we taped and watched the Jane Pauley show "Dateline NBC." It was called "Great Expectations" — of two young men growing up with a disability. The two young men were Jason Kingsley (me) and my friend Mitchell Levitz. I was so inspirative.... It showed me going to school, talking about my car, playing Nintendo, playing baseball and singing in Wig 'n' Whiskers. In that time I didn't sing well enough, not as well as I do now.

It showed me and Mitchell writing a book together. It is about people growing up with a disability, with Down syndrome.... After the Jane Pauley Show, Harcourt Brace called up and said they would be happy to publish that book. I will soon be a published author and we are going to get an editor and a spell checker and a person who will put us into chapters and the binders, the covers and put it into book form. And then it will be in the bookstores and the libraries. The first library I think will be in my school. And when I get to my job in my library, I can take out a book on disabilities and guess what book I am taking out? My book!

After I graduate from high school, I want to have a job being a teacher's aide, teaching little kids. I think I would be good at it. I like little kids.

I want to get married, to have my deductions and get a wife (named Tami) and live in the apartment. I have to pay for my electric bills, my life insurance, my car insurance, my Social Security, my Income Tax, food and clothes and some toys because I am planning to have my own kid. Fall in love and make history. And I have to pay my Miscellaneous, checks to pay for my baby-sitter for the baby so I can go out with my wife.

Now I am experiencing my independence to my parents to see how much things I could learn from them and from my experience. I will always work hard to keep my apartment and to be a good hard worker and to live my future life to make an accomplishment for all people to be proud of me.

*May '93*

**Jason:** Now in the present time this is the year 1993 and I'll tell you how it feels to be an uncle for my nieces and my nephews.

My brother Todd is married to my sister-in-law Michelle and I got two nieces and a nephew. Their names are Samantha, Rebecca, and the newcomer Jack. My other brother Glenn got divorced and now he is married to Jennifer. Glenn has two kids who is my other niece and nephew. They are Samara and Ethan, [who] is sometimes called Boomer.

The way I feel about my nieces and nephews is more than real important about my life. It makes me feel calm and it makes me feel that these are the kids that I would be happy to teach some day in the future, . . . a lot of stuff just as my grandpa did to me.

I love to be an uncle and I hope I will be the greatest model to my nieces and my nephews. I feel that I will like to see my nieces and my nephews grow up and I'll be happy and proud with them.

---

**Jason:** When I was born, the obstetrician said that I cannot learn, never see my mom and dad and never learn anything and send me to an institution. Which I think it was wrong.

Today we were talking about if I could see my obstetrician and talk to him, here are the things I would say. . . .

I would say, "People with disabilities *can learn!*"

Then I would tell the obstetrician how smart I am. Like learning new languages, going to other foreign nations, going to teen groups and teen parties, going to cast parties, becoming independent, being . . . a lighting board operator, an actor, the backstage crew. I would talk about history, math, English, algebra, business math, global studies. One thing I forgot to tell the obstetrician is I plan to get a academic diploma when I pass my RCTs....

I performed in "The Fall Guy" and even I wrote this book! He never imagined how I could write a book! I will send him a copy...so he'll know.

I will tell him that I play the violin, that I make relationships with other people, I make oil paintings, I play the piano, I can sing, I am competing in sports, in the drama group, that I have many friends and I have a full life.

So I want the obstetrician will never say that to any parent to have a baby with a disability any more. If you send a baby with a disability to an institution, the baby will miss all the opportunities to grow and to learn...and also to receive a diploma. The baby will miss relationships and love and independent living skills. Give a baby with a disability a chance to grow a full life. To experience a half-full glass instead of the half-empty glass. And think of your abilities not your disability.

I am glad that we didn't listen to the obstetrician...We will send a copy of this book to [him] and say, "See page 27." I wonder what he will say. I wonder if he will come to us and call us and what is his response, and we hope he would say that he made a mistake. His emotional feelings is...sorry, depressed, and mistakened.... He will never discriminate with people with disabilities again.

And then he will be a better doctor.

# 3

## Our Friendship

### "It Will Always Be There"

*June '92*

**Mitchell:** If you look at me and Jason, you'll see there are some things we have in common and some things that are different...like, for example, we both have the same disability and we both have problems and we also are in the same school district. Part of being in common with Jason is part of being as close friends, which is very significant, very important—

**Jason:** Very meaningful.

**Mitchell:** We are taking the same exams*...and therefore both of us have passed those exams. As well, we may have different friends, or we may have different views about with regarding the future and with regarding how we want our life the way it is.

**Jason:** And what about some different views about the book?

**Mitchell:** That's another thing.

**Jason:** Like my experiences are different from Mitchell and that's how we'll put it in the book. I'm in the middle of high school and Mitchell's been graduated. So our personality changes....

---

*New York State Regents Competency Tests

**Barbara:** Do you think your personalities are the same?

**Jason:** Physical yes...but not emotional. Emotional means how we feel about each other. We may have different ideas, different dreams.

**Mitchell:** If you ask my perspective about that, about personality, sometimes personality can change and everybody doesn't have the same personality. They can change how they feel about each other and how compatible they are...when regarding what kind of friends they are.

**Barbara:** You mentioned earlier, Jason, about personalities. I think sometimes people can become friends if they have things in common or similar personalities. I don't know how you two would describe your personalities. Maybe you can describe your personalities. Maybe we can see if you do have things in common.

**Mitchell:** In general I know what personalities are.

**Barbara:** Mitchell, why don't you describe Jason's personality as you see it. And Jason, you describe Mitchell's personality.

**Jason:** Mitchell is good, very fun to be with, serious, philosophical, grown up, mature, independent, and I can see that he's almost connected to me as a brother as a friend.

**Mitchell:** In my perspective, I see Jason as a fun-loving, gentle young man with a lot of talent and capabilities, able to be mature in a lot of areas. He is also a wonderful friend. He's wonderful by giving his perspective and opinion about things and I think very highly of Jason because he has a lot of talents, a lot of interests in things. I think Jason has a bright future ahead in his life.

[*to Jason*] What I'm trying to say is, you have great talents. You can do a lot of things. Not only being on TV — but the way you express yourself, the way you are with other people. Those are the talents. You're always open-minded and your heart is always open toward the people you care about.

**Jason:** Well, yeah. That's me all right.

**Barbara:** We were talking about similarities and differences today. Are there things in both of your experiences growing up that were similar? And some things in your growing up that were different?

**Mitchell:** If you look at both Jason's and my experiences, there are differences in the way we were grown up. Jason was born with two brothers, and I was born with two sisters. We feel differently about our families, about certain things, and we feel that there are different things that . . . are difficult to discuss with them. Both of our education is somewhat the same because we took mainstream courses and special ed courses. I mean, the program was the same, but we were in two different schools in the same district with different students.

**Barbara:** Talk about some other experiences you had growing up that were similar or different.

**Mitchell:** One of them that was quite different in the way we handled our problems and the people we asked to solve our problems. When I was in high school, my two sisters were there and I went to them with my problems and the dean of students and my teachers. Jason, who were the people you went to if you had problems?

**Jason:** Well it's hard to say because first of all easy problems I can work out myself . . . but hard problems I go to my psychologist, my parents, my friends and my family, the friends of my parents and I got many friends and family I can talk to if I have problems. . . .

**Mitchell:** Specifically in school, who do you talk to when you have problems?

**Jason:** In big problems in school, I can talk to the guidance [counselor], the teacher, kids who know me that care about me or adults that like me, or I can deal with the person who I am having problems to work things out with each other.

**Mitchell:** To compare me and Jason, we are quite different.

Physically, I'm much stronger in standing out with a message. My voice is louder than Jason's. We look different.

Among all the things that both me and Jason have in common or have differences in, nothing [can] change the way we feel about each other. The things, the way we feel about what we have in common in, we share those things throughout the time we have with each other.

But the things that we have differences in, is... because sometimes people take things differently. But to be logical, that the most important thing is that we should be compatible and enjoy the time that we have and to be friends with each other.

*November '92*

**Mitchell:** I'm interested in your feelings about our friendship since we began working on this book together.

Over the couple of years when we were in the process of doing this book, we've been giving our perspective and our opinions about a lot of the situations and a lot of topics.

To me it's very significant the way we feel about each other because, even though that we have a lot of differences regarding different opinions, but I do feel that regarding our friendship it's a vital important part between you and me.

Certain things I look up to you for.... Certain things you look up to me about. I remember once you asked me my advice when you had problems. And I asked your advice when I had problems. It's a two-way street. Then I felt that we both were helping each other to resolve our problems by doing that.

What I don't understand is where we put our friendship now. Should we continue having this friendship, or should we put it on hold? I don't want to jeopardize our friendship.

I think this book is so important for people who read this book to realize we are two different people. By giving two different perspectives, they might wonder how we became friends. We know each other throughout our life. We've been with each other many years.

**Jason:** You want me to state my feelings toward you. Well, here's the answer. The answer is that I feel warm-hearted to you. I think that what we should do for friendship is to keep having a relationship.

I hadn't been in your experiences quite yet because you're born three years earlier than me. The point of this book is we need a perception of the balance of our experience....

**Mitchell:** I understand what you're saying and I appreciate your feelings for me, but there's something else that is very relevant to the subject. A long time ago, when you were born. When Emily had you, the first person she contacted was my parents when you were born.

...Between you and me, we have a lot of differences in what we do and we have a lot in common. But we shouldn't base it on our disability. We should base it on the way we feel about each other and how both of our families got involved to help other people with disabilities as well because it had an impact not only on our friendship but on *their* friendship, too.

In the future where we're going with our friendship, I still want to continue this friendship that we have. Sometimes I feel that I'm not always there for you because I'm with other friends. I do care about you as a friend, and I want to continue being friends. Sometimes that you have expectations about me and I'm not always there all the time.

Regarding the future, I think that we will continue having a friendship. I feel our relationship is very important to both of us. I'm sure you feel the same way because our friendship is so important that we do not want to overlook any circumstance or anything of a shadow of a doubt because to me the very important thing about our friendship that makes it special is how we help each other out. The way we listen to each other and how we really feel about each other and that will give the people an impression about two different people with the same disability who have a friendship and will continue that friendship.

That will give us an interesting situation that how we figure the future will be for each other. Because we both have different plans for the future. I plan to see myself in government
or in a corporation, and you see something else. We have two
different things we want to do in the future, but the whole
thing is no matter what the future may be, our friendship will
always be there....

# 4
# **Having Down Syndrome**
## "There's More to It Than I Expected"

*August '90*

**Mitchell:** I wish I didn't have Down syndrome because I would be a regular person, a regular mainstream normal person. Because I didn't know I had Down syndrome since a long time ago, but I feel very special in many ways. I feel that being with, having Down syndrome, there's more to it than I expected. It was very difficult but... I was able to handle it very well.

**Jason:** I'm glad to have Down syndrome. I think it's a good thing to have for all people that are born with it. I don't think it's a handicap. It's a disability for what you're learning because you're learning slowly. It's not that bad.

There's a lot of things I did a lot of other people don't do. Like being in two different shows, going to a lot of conventions, award ceremonies like the Kennedy's,* and I'm a famous actor. First of all, when I was three, that's when I started to be in the show "This Is My Son." ... When I was three through sixteen I was filming "Sesame Street."

Six years before, when I was ten, I filmed "The Fall Guy." I

---

*The Kingsleys received the Joseph P. Kennedy Special Achievement Award for Families in July 1990.

got to learn a sixty-four-page script. How can a Down syndrome kid can memorize a sixty-four-page script? But I did it. In "The Fall Guy" I acted with Lee Majors....

I want to show people how I can count in many foreign languages and how I know my address when I was little. In "The Fall Guy" I am teaching Lee Majors how to count in three foreign languages: Spanish, French, and Japanese.

I guess some parents took their child to our house to talk about how...good...I am. To talk about Down syndrome and their baby. And how do you expect that child's future. And then they see me, how tall I am, how smart I am; and how nice I am and how friendly I am...and after a while, a couple of days, for all the things that I have done,...their decision for their baby to come to their house and have their parents. They feel happy about their baby because of me. That makes me feel proud that I helped them a lot.

### *July '90*

**Jason:** The most important thing you have to do with a new baby is take care of it. You have to teach them things step by step so they can learn more easily. You have to love them and hug them and kiss them every once in a while. You sing some songs to the baby. You have to feed them with milk and keep them clean and change their diapers. Just like any baby. If the baby has Down syndrome you have to try to help them more. You do more singing, more talking, more walking, more teaching, and more showing them around the house.

### *October '90*

**Mitchell:** I feel like the black sheep of the family. Because I think because my family might not have this burden except for me.

On a serious note, Dad, when you found out you had a boy and you found out I had Down syndrome, how did you reacted? How did you respond?

**Jack:** Well, I cried. Big time. I was very upset.

**Jason** [*to his father*]: How do you feel about me that I had Down syndrome when I was born?

**Charles:** Well, I cried, too. I think the reason I cried was I didn't know anything about Down syndrome. I didn't even know the words *Down syndrome* at that time. I'd heard them, but I didn't know what they meant.

When you were born, people that had Down syndrome didn't have a lot going for them. But you guys were two of the first kids in this country that started to let people know that people with Down syndrome could learn, could be bright, could be funny, sweet, could be charming, could be terrific kids. I gotta tell you guys, both of you, if it wasn't for you two, both your mothers and both your fathers would be very different people today. We wouldn't be nearly as helpful as we are if it hadn't been for the fact that we grew as you guys grew.

*June '92*

**Mitchell:** I am quite interested in knowing what your feelings are about me when I was born with Down syndrome.

**Jack:** Well, the interesting thing was, that you probably don't know about, when Mommy was student-teaching during college, teaching special ed, there were a few kids in her class with Down syndrome. They had class trips, and I used to go with her and we used to talk.

When you're getting married, you talk about your plans, and we had said that sometime after we had our regular family we'd like to adopt a child with Down syndrome.

When you were born, the news was devastating. I thought I wouldn't have anyone to help me cut the grass or shovel the snow. And since you were my first son, I immediately thought about the Bar Mitzvah and I thought you wouldn't be able to have a Bar Mitzvah. So even though I had once wanted to adopt a child with Down syndrome, I didn't expect you to be born with Down syndrome. So that was my reaction.

**Mitchell:** I disagree about what you said about adopting a child who has Down syndrome. That has me puzzled. It puzzles me, why did you thought that before I came along you wanted to adopt a child with Down syndrome before you even knew that I came along in your life?

**Charles:** Dad touched on it when he said he did volunteer work when your mom was teaching. He evidently *liked* kids with Down syndrome. Even before he knew you, he realized there was something special about them.

**Jack:** Even assuming you could not do a lot of the things you can do, we still thought someone with Down syndrome was very special and someone we'd like to have as part of our family.

*March '91*

**Jason:** Mom, I have a very important question for you. There are two kinds of people. There are people without Down syndrome in the normal outside world...and there are people *with* Down syndrome in the normal outside world. How can a special person with Down syndrome be in the normal outside world?

**Emily:** Why *shouldn't* a person with Down syndrome be in the normal outside world? *You* are a special person with Down syndrome, and you are in the normal outside world, aren't you?

**Jason:** Yes, on some occasions.

———

**Jason:** I think about this world that there is so much disaster, and I wish it would change.

**Emily:** What kind of disaster are you referring to?

**Jason:** Well, when I'm in school, I write slowly and when I write fast my writing comes sloppy and people don't understand my writing.... When I'm slow I keep behind...about my work. After the bell rings when I do my work, I may not be finished and do the things for homework which I hate to do at home. I'm lucky because I'm doing my homework at lunchtime and at study hall. If the bell rings from there, what can I do? I just have to do it at home, and I hate that.

I'm very slower than anyone. I'm slower than most people. Some people may be faster than I am, and some people may be slower than me. I wish I was faster....

**Emily:** Nobody else in your class has Down syndrome. Do you think they understand what Down syndrome is all about?

**Jason:** No. Actually some of the experts of Down syndrome may not know that I have Down syndrome. They only have to find out by themselves, just by reading this book.

**Emily:** Do you think that the kids in your class know you have some kind of disability?

**Jason:** I really don't know. It would be surprising to me that they know what kind of disability I have.

**Emily:** So nobody has ever told them about Down syndrome, right?

**Jason:** I believe so.

**Emily:** Do you think someone should tell them about you?

**Jason:** Yes, some people should teach them about Down syndrome. Then they could understand better or hope for the best or they could read this book about it....

### May '91

**Jason:** Mom, I have to tell you something about this life. I have a serious problem.

Some people are faster and some people are slower. I want them to stop so I can catch up. I don't want teachers to go faster than I am, too. I want people to have the same pace as I do. I want everyone to be the same, to learn the same.

I know I'm improving my disability, but I still have it. I may not be able to learn things and that makes me have a hard time. I still have the disability. How I want it to get away.

**Emily:** I wish I could make it go away.

**Jason:** The only way to make the disability go away is to have people treat me differently — warmly and close and affectionate. Like loving. People have their same feelings and love with me, too.

When kids are busy and teachers are marking grades, I'm alone with no other people to help. I'd like to have more friends — to share and get together with and have fun and even to help me study more.

I want this disability have to go away. I want to be just like everybody else.

*February '91*

**Mitchell:** I like being on TV a lot. It gives the viewers more chance to understand a person with a disability. I enjoy TV.... I believe I may be a good actor, but I really believe with my experience I could provide my own experience to tell the viewers how important and special a person with a disability is. And to have a better understanding all about having a disability.

I want to tell them that it is important that the person with a disability may have difficulties to understand and to let the viewers or the people know that they have to show some respect for them and to show how much they care about them. Because it's important for people to get feedback.... It's important to speak out because that would give them a chance to tell people how they feel about having the disability. It's important for them to explain to people what kind of a person I am.

**Jason:** That's why I want to be on TV. I really want to show that disabled people deserve respect from the viewers.

**Mitchell:** It's wonderful for parents to see disabled children on TV a lot. It could benefit them by realizing how important it is to have hope and faith. They could benefit watching "Sesame Street," watching kids who have disabilities on the show because it could give them some encouragement to do activities, become part of the community themselves. This could benefit the parents because they could be pleased and happy to see their children be involved, and that will give them hope for the future if their children watch the show.

**Jason:** For education, for school, what to expect for their child's future. He can go to school, and learn vocabulary and learn letters and alphabet and numbers which they teach on "Sesame Street."

*June '91*

**Mitchell:** What were your feelings about the taping and the interview with Jane Pauley?*

**Jason:** I'll give you two reasons why my feelings were positive about this taping and the interview. One was because I wanted to teach the people in this world, to benefit what they're doing, about what our experiences are. And second, I want all of the people to understand me.... I feel blessed and happy about it.

**Mitchell:** At the interview with Jane Pauley I thought I had everything in a smooth rhythm operation. Even though Jane Pauley is hot, sexy, and attractive, I felt I was very easygoing and I told her how I felt. Publicly.

**Emily:** Did you tell her she was hot, sexy, and attractive?

**Mitchell:** No, I didn't tell her that. I also thought that the questions that she asked were very on target. The questions were very important, and I told her I was interested down the road five to ten years from now that I plan to run for president of the United States. And she said that had a good ring to it.

...She asked me, "When you run for president, what will you want to do?" I told her that I want to help the people with disabilities out so they can be recognized even more and help them and ... to fix up the national budget. Which of course, we need a budget of course.

Besides those two, I told her that I met Governor Cuomo at a dinner for Special Olympics, the dinner in honor of Jason. I told her that I am mixed feelings about Governor Cuomo now

---

*Aired on the premiere episode of "Dateline NBC," March 31, 1992

because of the reasons of the way he's handling the budget and these outrageous cuts to the schools and what he's doing to WARC.

I was going to ask Jason about the interview with Jane Pauley. How he felt about the interview.

**Jason:** Well, for my interview with Jane Pauley, I was calm and relaxed. We talked about school and work and my job and what I'm doing for my summer and next year, what I'm going to achieve for next year's school. And a lot of other things. Jane Pauley was a very outgoing lady. I felt blushed by it. I thought she was attractive and the most pretty I ever talked to. [Other] people I have interviewed with are not as pretty as Jane Pauley.

### *August '91*

**Jason:** Our Christmas card next year is going to show me voting. That I can vote. I'm teaching about many different disabled kids can vote because I have a disability, too. . . .

**Mitchell:** Sometimes people will get the message if they see them in action. A picture can tell a lot. Actions does more than words. In reality you have to see the person in firsthand seeing that they can do it. From the perspective of TV viewers, people will get the message if you go on the air, live or TV or radio, and tell them the message.

**Emily:** That's exactly why we were so excited about the Jane Pauley show. Because it showed you two guys doing some very exciting and independent things. And that will get to millions and millions of people with a very positive message about what people with Down syndrome are capable of.

**Jason:** People over the world should watch.

**Mitchell:** That's true. It also gives the perspective for the TV viewers to see how important these people are, and it makes a difference to see what they're doing in the perspective of what they see.

And also the other part is that running for office — because what I can do is — the more publicity I get, the better advantage that that will give me. People will have to see me in action.

What I'm doing is, I'm thinking that I want to, sometime, go down to Washington, D.C., see President Bush myself before and to tell him that I will make a statement sending out a message that there are special people out there, who needs your help, get your respect... to listen to them and tell them how important that we need the help. We already have services that are provided, but we feel that there is more to life and we should express those feelings out, and that's the basic reason why I want to go to Washington, D.C., and make that statement.

**Jason:** I may go with you. Because I want to get a statement not just to the nation but to the whole world, the continents. The whole world needs a national holiday called "Jason and Mitchell Are Working on a Project to Inform Many Different Kinds of People."

## *June '92*

**Emily:** The other day when we talked, you said you wished you were born without Down syndrome.

**Mitchell:** Yes, I feel really strongly about that. The reason I feel really strongly about it is I feel like I'm just like the other people — Bush, Kennedy, for example. I feel like that because I'm living independently away from my parents. I feel it is important to me that I want to have my life the way I want it to be.

Let's think of "Life Goes On." If we were born without Down syndrome, we'd have a life like Tyler.* There is a whole different world out there for a whole different group of people.

---

*A supporting character on the show who plays a popular high school student who's a good friend of Corky's

Not just a group of people with disabilities . . . and to me I want to be a part of that.

*December '92*

**Mitchell:** I think we should end this by stating that we should never call us Down syndrome.* We should call each other Up syndrome because Up syndrome would help each other out, being involved in communities because it's part of being Up syndrome.

**Jason:** Parts of being Up syndrome is the word Up. It means your positive side.

**Mitchell:** Up is positive, down is sad. There are two perspectives here. Down syndrome meaning a disability. Up syndrome meaning positive with a disability. It's a combination of things.

**Jason:** I think Up syndrome is positive with a disability and Down syndrome is, well, you're feeling depressed a little bit, going down. This Down syndrome is the wrong name of our disability. Down syndrome is no longer to be existed because now we have our talents and our experiences to learn things. Down syndrome will change to Up syndrome, and that will make the Down syndrome go away.

**Mitchell:** No, the disability never can change. We'll call it Change syndrome. Things change around if you think about it. The reason we should call it Change syndrome is we can't change the disability but we *can* change the way we feel.

**Jason:** Don't be in a low, grumpy attitude. The positive side of Up syndrome is to be proud of you, learn about it, how you do it, and be happy. Put it into actions. Be motivated. You can realize now: You can do everything yourself from now on.

---

*"Down syndrome" was named after Dr. John Langdon Down, who provided the first clinical description of this condition in 1866.

# 5
# At School
## "Easy Steps to Get to Hard Work"

*July '90*

**Jason:** Most of my classmates don't know that I have Down syndrome because they told me that I'm not going to learn this year. But when my parents came for Parents' Night, my classmates realized that Jason *can* do it and he has Down syndrome. So they gave me a chance to do it. And I did pretty well. I got the highest mark in history in the whole class. They didn't think I could make it, but I did. I got 89 in my history test.... I made honor roll because I got an 88 [average].

In shop there was one kid gave me a hard time. And that name was DJ. When I was erasing something, DJ came up to me and grabbed the eraser while I was erasing. That was rude what he did. I told the teacher and DJ got blamed. I told the principal the next day, and he thinks he wants to suspend DJ for what he did.

And there's another person who affected me whose name is Victor. Victor said, "Hey get away, you jerk." He called me, "Get the hell out of here, you ass." He thinks that I am retarded because I wasn't listening to what he was saying. He says, "What are you, retarded or deaf or something?" I said to him, "You, too. Get away." That didn't help me at all. He just said, "That's fine, have it your way." I just ignored him and got

away. He was a bully. He was trying to stop me every time I
see him. But I was smart. That was the wrong thing for him to
do when I am on my way to my next class.

People who are teasing me, they think they are cool, but
they aren't. I felt worried at first. Then I got mad. Then I was
disappointed. And sad. People who do the teasing don't know
that I have feelings. My feelings got hurt. I am trying to tell the
kid to buzz off. That didn't help, so I ignored him.

I have lots of pressure in school. Very hard. I feel I work
harder than other kids. Other kids are getting work so fast.
My eyes are getting watery. I put the pencil down and with
my two fists try to punch someone in my imagination because the pressure when I'm doing my work. It's hard for me.
Looks like war. In my imagination. But I end up doing it. Slowly. I still have pressure but slowly. After I do it, I ask the teachers, "What is my grade for my test?" When they told me I got
a 99 on my final test and I feel almost quite happy and proud.
I say, "Thank you. Oh, I can't believe all that work and all
that pressure I have done it." I feel great when I do well on a
test.

Some other grades that I had: I got 88 on my shop test, 89
on my history test, 76 on my math test—that's kind of a good
grade, but I don't like it very much. Math was algebra. I
learned three different kinds of math which are called mean,
median, and mode. Science was chemistry at end of the year. I
learned all through electricity to chemistry in the eighth grade.
I learned protons, neutrons, and electrons. I learned the period-
ic table of elements. Don't you know for a fact there are 113
[sic] elements that are known.

...Next year I go to high school. Now all the kids know
that a kid with Down syndrome can be in high school. I hope
the kids will be more friendly. And some new kids that are
older or my age and more grown up. I might predict that some
kids might invite me to parties that have wine and beer and

drugs. I say, "No way Jose." I would prefer to go to parties that have Coke and potato chips and all that stuff. I would like to get invited to parties.

I expect the work in high school to be easy steps to get to hard work. With Down syndrome, I need to learn step by step. I think it's gonna turn out okay. I expect to make more friends and more respectful people.

In this program I'm in, I'm the only one who has a disability and never talk to any friends who don't have a disability because I'm still afraid and confused about that. Other kids do have learning problems, like one kid doesn't know how to spell, one kid doesn't know how to behave, one kid has trouble learning things. I'm the only person in that class who has Down syndrome.

**Mitchell:** In my experience, people will treat you unfairly because they don't understand a person with a disability as well as yourself and the teacher. The reason they treat you unfairly because they may take advantage of you and they may try to get you in trouble by doing many things that can cause you by hurting your feelings. And then you have to pay the consequences. . . . If there is a lot of peer pressure, they may think they can use you because you are very special. They may treat you differently because they can tell not only that you're special, they know they can make fun of you and that you'll get in trouble.

**Jason:** In middle school some kids are taking advantage for me looking forward to get trouble. They always fool around with me, calling names and calling curses and all that stuff. One kid says, "Hey you kid go way and leave me alone, you're not my friend, I don't like you." He's taking too much pressure on me and I know how to handle it. I just simply go and talk to my parents when I get home. Every once a week I go to the therapist and talk about these problems I had in school. Because some kids are making me a hard time learning and hard time to express my feelings about this whole thing about school is about.

### August '90

**Mitchell:** I had a problem playing soccer in high school.... I was immature. I did things that I embarrassed my two sisters because of their friends....

One of the immature things I did was I made up raps about women and I say out loud on the bus, going to our games, to away games. They were laughing at me when I would do this, and I felt I was being too immature.

I was [just] doing it for fun...just to get attention. I got the attention.... The result was my sisters would be embarrassed to hear all this—all these things which I done. My sisters would be very annoyed, and on some occasions as I recall they said that they come up to me and talk about it. They tell me first. And not go to my parents. Then confronting my parents. They would say not to do it again, they felt embarrassed and they do not want to feel embarrassed because of my immaturity.

**Barbara:** How did you work this out?

**Mitchell:** I worked this out by talking about it and by acting mature. I had help from my sister, my parents, the dean, and a school psychologist. I would talk to them and try a solution. This went through soccer season.

### October '90

**Barbara:** Do you make believe you don't have Down syndrome? Is that why you don't hang around with kids with disabilities?

**Mitchell:** Yes.... I don't know how to say this—but I'd rather think of myself as normal than as a disability.

In school, the guys I hang around with, I earn their respect. I want to be part of the gang. I want to put my disability on the side and the cool side of me out...and then I think of myself as normal....

*August '90*

**Mitchell:** Sometimes when I'm in school, they see how I'm acting toward other students, or acting toward the staff, they could see that my personal relationship with the other people are more important. But they don't see that. They [try] to get me instigated. Because I easily get into trouble. When I was in ninth grade, for example, I would do a lot of immature things. Like [once] I pulled the fire alarm and got suspended for five days. Because they were telling me to do it. I just was doing it for the fun of it to get attention.

The important thing to learn, when you start high school, you should start off on the right step. Meet friends who could understand you and how you feel, according to your feelings, and you can say to the dean or to your psychologist that you have some problems that you need to talk to them. It's always good to talk to your psychologist. He can give you advice about what you can do in a situation that's hard for you to get out of. Because they would probably build you up into a way that they would try to influence you in a way to do something that is wrong. But you have to prove to yourself. Should I do it or not? Question is, Are you strong enough to tell the people who bug you to stop or not?

**Jason:** I think I'm strong enough to tell them, "Hey stop it you bastard."

**Mitchell:** That might go toward a fight. Once you get into a fight, then the dean or the psychologist would get involved.

**Jason:** I would say, "Would you stop that a minute? I have to talk to the guidance counselor about you."

**Mitchell:** They will try to get you in trouble. Talk behind your back. Say things that might hurt you emotionally.

**Jason:** If they follow me in my back, trying to fight with me, then I'll have to ask the nearest caring, understandable person to deal with that guy.

*June '92*

*The following piece was written by Mitchell.*

Being in Walter Panas High School with Leah and Stephanie helped me to get through high school. They were there to talk to me when I had problems with other students, or with my classes they would help me study for tests or exams.... Both Leah and Stephanie understood my problems. For example, when I was influenced to set off the fire alarm [one time], I was suspended for five days.... I can understand that this was very serious, but I was able to behave myself for the rest of the year. Both of my sisters were there to tell me not to listen to those people because they can get you into serious trouble. By having both of them there, they helped me realize that I can make friends who understand me for who I am....

*June '91*

**Mitchell:** Last Saturday the graduation of Walter Panas High School was very successful.

The graduation felt very important to me. It meant that I achieved a lot. With a lot of support and guidance from my family and from my friends and that I could make it up to this point....

When I received the diploma and the awards, it meant very important to me because I was recognized as a student who had achieved a lot. Throughout my high school career I felt a lot of feelings inside about myself.... The graduation ceremony...helped me to recognize that I have a future. A future that will build to a dream.

This is the end of one part of the saga of a book. Now I'm entering a new phase, and the new phase is called "The Future and the Dream." With that in mind, my intent is to achieve a future that will help myself to benefit from my high school career.

When I got the standing ovation from my fellow students and from the families, I felt very proud of myself that I achieved a lot. I felt that I really improved and that people understood and cared about me.

**Jason:** I felt proud of my friend Mitchell, gave the standing ovation for the three awards [a community service award, the dean's award, and a commendation from the state assembly]. It helps me to benefit so I can graduate after when I have a senior year. Mitchell helped me a lot. And I felt proud at the graduation.

**Mitchell:** Those awards meant that I achieved a lot. It was recognizing my excellence and achievement in helping the community. That I helped this community out a lot. The dean's award for helping the dean out a lot of times, to support him and how much work I put into to help him to be a wonderful friend.

**Jason:** . . . If I work hard in *my* dean's office, I might get the dean's award, too. If I work hard with dictionaries and encyclopedias and put into alphabetical order, I'd be a beneficial of a business award. And I might get the Wig 'n' Whiskers [Drama Club] award. And probably also I'd get a teacher's award by helping the teachers to clean up the books at the end of the year and to keep everything in place and nice and neat for the next year.

**Mitchell:** What Jason said . . . in order to receive an award, you have to be recognized by the community and the school. It's what you do in the community that helps the people. Basically my prediction is that Jason might get an award for his academic achievements in class, in school.

It doesn't make sense in my mind that what he predicted in a business award and what he said. I have a feeling that it's better to recognize Jason as a most improved student. So that you can reflect on all of the work that you accomplished with the help and support you got from your family and the school.

**Jason:** As you said about being the most improved student, getting an academic award, you don't mean that I'd get an award for English or history. That's part of academics. What part should I get? Speech or English? Math or history?

**Mitchell:** It depends on the marks that you get. Jason, this is just a prediction. We don't know until it happens.

I got an academic award in English. It's not at graduation, but it is an award that I achieved from the hard work which I put into the class. It was the highest average in English in the class. And last year I got an award for achievement in business.

They do the underclassmen awards the day of the senior breakfast. I don't know about Lakeland High School. I couldn't speculate how they do it at Lakeland....

**Emily:** You had a huge fabulous party to celebrate your graduation. How many people were there?

**Mitchell:** Approximately 150.

**Jason:** I think I counted them 165.

**Mitchell:** ... Harry Greenberg gave the introduction and gave a speech and read the letter from Congressman Fish. He read a letter to recognize myself for the achievements which I done. In honor of that, at the Capitol they will raise a flag in honor of my graduation. Then I will be receiving the flag.

**Emily:** Did you know that Jason has a flag just like that? It was flown over the U.S. Capitol in honor of his appearance on "The Fall Guy." It's hanging in his room.

**Barbara:** You guys have another thing in common!

**Jason:** Mitchell and I are *all* in common.

### January '93

**Jason:** Mitchell, I want your advice of what courses you've been taking when you were my age.... What kind of courses were you taking to prepare for your future?

**Mitchell:** To be honest with you, Jason, when I was in high school I took business courses. I took U.S. government and economy.... It was very difficult at times. But to me it was easy to understand because I keep up in the world, what's been happening in the world and what's happening in the newspaper. My advice to you is do what you think is best. By using your best instincts, by determining what courses to take, it's your decision to make.

[*to Barbara & Emily*] What I'm interested in is different [from] what Jason is interested in. We have two different backgrounds and two different things we want to do in our future.

**Jason:** Like we're in two different fields.

**Mitchell:** Right. That's why we have to see, we have some similarities but we have to differentiate your goals in the future and my goals in the future might be two different things. You tell me your goal, and I'll tell you my honest opinion of that.

**Barbara:** Part of what you did your senior year in high school, Mitchell, besides taking some courses to prepare you and some courses for fun, you also spent some time working in the school, getting some real work experience.

**Mitchell:** In rebuttal of what you said, it's not that I took courses in work.... What I did in school was...like I helped the dean of students for four years, Mort David, as his assistant. I answered his phone. I did his mail for him. I'd go and get a student for him when he needs to speak to them. I did a lot of things for him so that he'd be able to do what he needed to get done, which was a great asset to him.

**Emily:** Jason, you're doing some things like that, too. You're working two days a week in the school library. That's a work experience.

**Jason:** That's a work experience I have right now in my junior year. What we're exploring right now is being in senior year. What the senior year will be like. What courses would you think that I should take?

**Mitchell:** I could give you some suggestions off the bat. For example, continue working in the library. That's very important. Since you enjoy the theater, see if there's a course in that. Since you're in Wig 'n' Whiskers, that would be a great asset, too.

**Jason:** My core classes are history, English, science, and math. I would like to do some work experiences in that to go up to my goal to be a teacher's aide. Some of my courses I might take during my academic year might be helping the children.... There's a course called Preparation for Marriage.

Actually child psychology is mainly about behavior with humans and children. Somehow that will be true, but I don't think it's enough to take that course. Child behavior...

**Emily:** They have an actual preschool where you could work as part of your work experience.

**Jason:** I would like that.

**Mitchell:** The parallel between Jason and my sister Stephanie that she is studying child psychology. Her major is early childhood education and family studies and counseling.

**Jason:** Family studies I'm not quite sure of, but early childhood is a part I like....

**Mitchell:** Children with learning disabilities?

**Jason:** Just plain old children. I may have a variety: black and white, disabled and nondisabled, Down syndrome and non–Down syndrome.

**Mitchell:** The reason I brought it up is interesting to me. To me, we both have a disability. It might be difficult for people like us.... There are certain skills that we are capable of doing and certain skills that we are not because of the disability that we have. For example, let's say myself. I see myself being in politics. Some of the skills that politicians have might be easy for them but difficult for me. I might not have the skills to be a politician because I might not have the skills you need.

**Jason:** So long as you learn them.

**Mitchell:** It takes a long time to learn them.

**Jason:** You can learn them anyway—even if it takes a long time.

**Emily:** Do you think, Jason, that there are some skills that you guys don't have because of your disability which will make certain jobs too difficult to do?

**Jason:** No. As long as I learn them, as long as teachers keep teaching me, it's no problem. No job is too hard for us to do. A teacher's aide might be hard for a person my age but as long as I learn to do it with a teacher.

Any job I can do, if I can learn.

**Barbara:** Let's look at this course, Early Childhood Education: [*Reading from high school course book*] "Throughout the year you will plan activities and work closely with children in a preschool setting. Students are trained for employment in child development and related fields." That's the way you get a chance to find out if you like it and if you're good at it.

**Jason:** If I'm good at it, can I do it the rest of the day?

**Emily:** You'd work with actual children part of the day, and you'd get credits for it toward your diploma. The rest of the day you'd do your academics.

**Barbara:** It's like trying it out to see if you like to do it.

**Jason:** If I like it, can I do it all day?

**Emily:** After you graduate you can get a full-time job and do it full-time.

**Jason:** Preparation for Marriage is another course. Cooking skills, vacuuming skills . . .

**Emily:** I think the Preparation for Marriage course is more about values and relationships and commitment than vacuuming.

**Jason:** Preparation for Marriage is like preparing for independence. What skills you need to learn before your step to get married. And emotional skills, too. You can squeeze it all in one.

I'm right now into more independence. What's more important than being an independent person when you're preparing for marriage?

**Barbara:** That course covers teenage marriage, male/female relationships, economics of marriage, and mate selection. It's also about picking the right person to marry. They have guest speakers, movies, and classroom discussions to talk about different aspects of marriage. It's only for seniors.

**Jason:** I'll take that.

# 6
# **Having Fun**
## "I Feel Happy and Hoppy"

*October '92*

**Mitchell:** Entertainment covers a lot of territory. Such as... films, music, television shows, and what goes on behind the sets and what do we enjoy of what we see or what we hear in the entertainment field.

**Emily:** What are your favorite kinds of music?

**Mitchell:** That's hard to say, but I can say I like all kinds of music. Like slow, soul and rock, and the oldies. Like about in the seventies and the sixties.

**Jason:** What about the forties?

**Mitchell:** How about jazz and western?

**Jason:** Western is about the 1800s.

**Mitchell:** There's all kinds of western music that's out now.

**Jason:** I like classical music. Also 1960s, pop (like 1970s), rap and rock and roll (1980s), Broadway shows (anytime), Nelson Eddy I love (that's 1940s). Gilbert and Sullivan. Birthday songs. Christmas carols. Hanukkah carols.

Any kind of love songs I like, too. On a tape once I made a collection of love songs. Like "People Will Say We're in Love" from *Oklahoma!*, "Me and My Girl" from *Me and My Girl*....

Many songs have a lot of emotion to it. Take pop for

instance. I feel happy and hoppy when I hear pop music. If I like to listen to love songs, it makes me sweet and blushed.

**Mitchell:** The main reason why I like the music I hear is because that I enjoy it and it is fun to listen to it. Certain music makes me feel the way I do feel, which is sometimes conflicts certain things. For example, sometimes when I listen to a song that's very slow, I might feel very sad or upset because it might remind me of certain things that happen in the world.

Part of being in the music industry targets what the fans like and what they enjoy. And that ties in to the way I feel about the music I hear, ties me into being a fan of certain artists or performers. Some of them including Debbie Gibson, Michael Jackson, and Madonna, who is now under controversy. But in any case, there are many others, many people which I like. It would take a long time by naming every single performer.

**Jason:** I like—Beach Boys I like. Polka people. Tyne Daly in *Gypsy.* My favorite Broadway show character is Sky Masterson, from *Guys and Dolls.* My drama teacher from day camp was in *Pajama Game.* He played the guy who sings "Hey There."

**Emily:** If you could play any role in any Broadway show yourself, what role—

**Jason:** What do I choose? Well, I want to play Peter Pan. Yul Brynner played King of Siam. I would like to do that. Or Paul from *Carnival.*

Oh, I know! Tulsa! In *Gypsy.* I went on the stage when I was in my freshman year. We went [backstage] to visit Tyne when she was in *Gypsy* on Broadway and I saw the actor that played Tulsa who said he could teach me how to do tap dancing. I went out on the stage and I danced Tulsa's dancing. That was after the show was done. I did Tulsa-dancing right on the stage.

**Barbara:** Mitchell, you talked about the controversy about Madonna, about how performers can have influence on people. How do you feel about what Madonna does, and how that might affect people?

**Mitchell:** To certain degree that what a performer does has an impact and influence on other people. What makes them believe that if one person can do that, the other person can. Positively influence what may happen or may disrupt of the law. I mean certain things the law says....

I can give you an example. One of the songs is about sex. Now to me, sex is an issue should be made private. It should not be in the hands of the media, not be in the hands of any journalist. Because it's a matter of principle and that principle is choice. People have a choice to choose of what they like and what they dislike.

There is...not just Madonna...but that song about the police, killing police stuff. Some rapper. To me that all that stuff does create a lot of controversy because they want to create controversy so they can have the attention and influence society.

**Emily:** But what do you think should be done about that? Should people be prevented from singing certain kinds of songs? What does that say about our freedom of speech?

**Mitchell:** To me, freedom of speech is part of our rights, and those rights should not be taken away from us. That is the way we express ourselves. I would say no singer should refrain from singing a song because that is part of their freedom of speech.

The other part of this, what they're singing about, is making a choice. The choice should be made by the people who listen to the music. They are the ones who make the decision because that's where the controversy starts between what they like and what they don't like.

**Emily:** So you think the singer has the right to sing even if it's about killing cops, but the public has the right not to listen or not to buy those songs.

**Mitchell:** That's correct.

**Jason:** I think they should stop singing songs about killing cops. I just don't want the cops to be dead.

**Emily:** Do you think the songs will influence people?

**Jason:** I think the song will influence people to have more violence and kill cops. I don't want them to sing songs about killing cops. We need more subtle music.

**Mitchell:** What you're saying is you prefer the performers not to sing the songs because of what may happen.

**Jason:** Yes.

**Barbara:** Let's move on to television.

**Jason:** A lot of TV stars which I like . . . like Lee Majors, who was playing the part of "The Fall Guy," a stuntman. He is my pal. We went to the studio to see him and be in his show. . . .

**Mitchell:** What shows do you like to watch?

**Jason:** "Brady Bunch," "Full House," MTV, "America's Funniest Home Videos," "Life Goes On." I'm still grown to love "Sesame Street."

**Mitchell:** There's a lot of shows which I like to watch. The shows I like to watch are very realistic, and many people watch those shows because they have an impact on reality. The shows are "Life Goes On," "Full House," "Sixty Minutes," "Cosby Show," "A Different World," "Cheers."

**Jason:** Do you like to watch soap operas like "Loving" and "All My Children"? "General Hospital"?

**Mitchell:** When I'm home from work sometimes I do watch soaps. To name specifics, "Santa Barbara," "Days of Our Lives," and "Another World." Those shows are fiction. Basically I stick to the shows that are realistic that have impact on today, on life.

**Jason:** Don't you think soap operas have conversations that seem real? Like in "One Life to Live" they have conversations like what happened to one family. It made me feel like having a family just like that.

**Mitchell:** To me to a certain degree that soap operas can be realistic, but in some sense that they stick to story lines that they feel is important for the show. They want to get people interested in watching the shows.

The reality of television shows. If you look at every single show, which shows are more of a reality that is, that deals with issues that are happening today? I can name one of them that we all have common in: "Life Goes On." That show has a reality and proves to us that a show can be something that we all like. It's dealing with a family with one child has Down syndrome. Because to me, it is a reality to refer to that person with a disability has an impact of everyone else. Because people want to see reality... not fiction.

**Barbara:** How about people on the shows that you like?

**Mitchell:** I like Chris Burke. I like Bill Cosby and the people from "Beverly Hills, 90210." That's a show I like.

**Barbara:** Jason wants to talk about Kellie Martin [from "Life Goes On"].

**Jason:** Yeah!

**Mitchell:** Me too.

**Jason:** She's very sweet, very understandable, and she's a good comfortable girl to be with and talk to. And she's really a very comfortable kid. Both Becca and the actress Kellie Martin. Becca is relaxed with Corky, the same way as Kellie Martin to me.

**Barbara:** You think Kellie Martin is nice and relaxed with Chris Burke?

**Jason:** Yes. And I think Kellie Martin might be relaxed with other people, like me. She looks like a sister for me. A very close shivering glowing star. She's very shimmering and she's like an inspirative sister to me.

**Barbara:** Mitchell, do you want to talk about Kellie Martin and your real-life sister Leah?

**Mitchell:** They both have many things in common. One of the things they both have — they both wear glasses. They both has the same sense of humor and the same personality. It's not easy to tell them apart....

**Jason:** Who is that other girl that I also liked a lot? What about the girl with the blue bikini . . . on [that episode of] "Life Goes On." Miss January.

**Mitchell:** I know what you're talking about! The fantasy.

**Barbara:** What are the kinds of films you like?

**Mitchell:** It's a combination of things. To me I like a lot of movies. . . . I can name some specifics: action-packed movies, adventure, love. . . .

**Jason:** . . . Comedy, Broadway, science fiction. . . . Oh, I like horror, too.

**Mitchell:** I definitely like horror, too.

**Barbara:** You do?!

**Mitchell:** Mom, get into the 90s! Some favorites [are] movies with Tom Cruise, *Top Gun, Cocktail, Born on the Fourth of July, Far and Away, Dirty Dancing, Dances with Wolves, Silence of the Lambs, Beaches, Cape Fear* —

**Jason:** Ooooo I love that!

**Mitchell:** *Terminator II* —

**Jason:** What about *The Addams Family*?

**Mitchell:** *Wayne's World, Porky's* —

**Barbara:** Mitchell!

**Mitchell:** Mom, you're the one who brought up the subject! *Peggy Sue Got Married* —

**Jason:** *Ghost; Jungle Book; Gypsy; Neverending Story* Part 1 and 2; *Back to the Future* Parts 1, 2, and 3; *Scrooged*; Albert Finney musical version of *Scrooge; Peter Pan; Little Mermaid; The Outsiders; That Was Then, This Is Now; Bill & Ted's Excellent Adventure* and *Bogus Journey; Vice Versa; 18 Again; Like Father Like Son.* . . .

**Barbara:** How about things like concerts? That's a form of entertainment.

**Mitchell:** I like Debbie Gibson, Michael Jackson, Red Hot Chili Peppers, Guns N' Roses, Bon Jovi —

**Jason:** Wyld Stallions.

**Emily:** Now is that real or fantasy?

**Jason:** Fantasy. From Bill and Ted. How about New Kids On The Block . . . ?

**Mitchell:** I've gone to Debbie Gibson, Michael Jackson. One with my friends. One with my father. I enjoyed both of them a lot. I enjoyed both of the music which they sing. It's very noisy. People standing up dancing and having fun. Sometimes people take off their shirts. People buy stuff — like shirts, banners, all kinds of stuff. And programs, posters. I enjoy the music.

**Jason:** About concerts and music, kids like me and Mitchell can have fun by entertaining themselves, to have some fun and enjoyment of their lives. And I would recommend adults can also have fun.

It's not only they have to work, but I want them to spend more time with their kids to have fun with a lot of children.

**Mitchell:** People enjoy entertainment because they enjoy the pleasure and the fun and the interest in the field.

**Jason:** Shakespeare said "All the world's a stage and the people are nearly players" and any special place or time is the backstage crew. Our perceptions are cameras to look at the actors who play the characters so real.

———

**Jason:** What sports that I like doing or have done in the past? I like to play baseball in my backyard. We have a big can of balls. Sometimes Dad or sometimes my brothers pitch the ball. I hit. Sometimes I miss and sometimes I hit. One time with the kids around, I hit the roof of one car and made the alarm came on. I'm a very special hitter. . . . I might wish I was a good hitter just like Don Mattingly.

The things that I have done in my past was that I did track and field . . . in Special Olympics. In "Fall Guy" I did the fifty-meter dash. I did volleyball, tennis in my friend's backyard, I played soccer, with shin guards and one time the ball came onto my head and I got hurt.

Last year I did basketball. It's a good game....

After all the exercising and sports on land, we have a water-freshing sport called swimming, and I did that well, too. I did freestyle and breaststroke, and I learned how to do the backstroke. Sometimes I lose my breath toward the deep end, and sometimes my ears get clogged and I can't hear as well. But I always can beat my mom in a race.

**Mitchell:** When I was in high school, I played in soccer for one year with friends of mine. I also played the sport in the community with other people. I played soccer for many of years when I was young.

There was one game which I scored the winning goal. I scored, and people were proud that I did kick the ball into the net and they were excited for me.

**Jason:** ...Did the guys give you a hug or shake your hand or anything like that?

**Mitchell:** From what I can remember, they didn't hug me or anything. That would be inappropriate. They gave me high fives and shakes.

When I was playing soccer, I used to win trophies because the team been winning a lot of games. One summer I went to a soccer camp and I learned more about playing soccer. I was involved in a tournament in West Point when I was playing soccer. When I was older I was in a traveling league for AYSO.

I've also been involved in other sports as well. For example: tennis, baseball, football, swimming, Ping-Pong, downhill skiing, and waterskiing.

**Jason:** I did waterskiing once in camp. In Camp Northwood. I stood on the aquaplane, and I tried to stand on the skis but I lost grip and I went like flipping right over, like skid-skid-skid. I was trying to hold on to the bar as well as I could. The boat pulled me and the skis fell off and I got dragged along by the boat.

I played backgammon, which is a game which I tournament-played. We played "sick-dying-dead football." The rules are: once you missed one ball, you're sick. If you miss another, you're dying. If you miss the third time, you're dead and you drop on the floor.

I played football in my past in Copper Beech Middle School where I hit my wrist on the cement and it broke. That was the time of my field trip to Washington, D.C., with my cast on. I thought it was difficult to have a cast on because it's very hard to cut my meat that way. Like climbing up the statue in Washington, D.C. Somebody said I'm going to hurt my arm strongly if I climb up,... so I didn't. To keep it from getting wet, we had garbage bags with rubber bands to keep it tight so water won't go into my cast and make it wet.

Years back, when I was young in 1982, when I was eight, I have a counselor from Briarton Day Camp who came and taught me swimming. He was Larry. He taught me "long arms." He used to drag me around the pool and made me swim. And I said no no no no no no no! One time my arms was not long enough, so I got my arms long enough to do swimming and we had a ten-minute break at the end. It was so funny that my breakfast was caught in the top of my neck and I vomited into the pool. And then after that we went back to swimming. At the end of the lesson he taught me Swedish how to say "I love you" and count from one to ten in Swedish. He was a good pal.

**Mitchell:** Jason, what kind of sports do you like to *watch*?

**Jason:** I like to watch baseball and football, sometimes golf. My favorite team in baseball is the Yankees and the Pittsburgh Pirates and Toronto. I like the Yankees.

**Mitchell:** From what I remember, one summer you, myself, and two other people took a picture with Don Mattingly for a magazine. I said [to Don Mattingly], "Is your bat corked?" He said no and laughed.

**Jason:** The funniest thing about me taking a picture with Don Mattingly—I started to walk away with his bat and Don Mattingly said, "Wait! It has all my hits in that bat!" So I kissed the bat and gave it back to him, and he got a single and a double and a homer with that bat in that game. Then he signed the bat for me and he give it to me. He gave me also an autographed hat of the Yanks.

**Mitchell:** I also got a ball with all the Yankee team players. Every player from the team. And Don Mattingly signed my glove, too.

**Jason:** I didn't love Don Mattingly as my only one person. I started to have many fans on many teams. In Pittsburgh Pirates, I like Drabek, Van Slyck. In the Mets, I like Gregg Jefferies, Darryl Strawberry. In Atlanta, I like Terry Pendleton and there's a tennis champion at the MBIA Invitational [Municipal Bond Investors Assurance Corporation] I saw named Sam Jones. Except he's a basketball player.

Every year I go to MBIA with my family. The MBIA [Invitational Golf Tournament] is to contribute money for Westchester ARC and Special Olympics. Jack Butler and Dad started the MBIA [Invitational]. They are chairmen. I make a lot of speeches at MBIA. I want to show the people how wonderful I am, how smart I am, and what makes me a grateful person.

**Mitchell:** When my sister Leah and Saul were going out, he took us to a basketball game with the Knicks. When we were sitting on the lower deck, I saw Saul managed to get Patrick Ewing's wristband and after he got the wristband, he gave it to me. So I put it on my wrist and I kept it there. I liked it a lot.

I like a lot of teams, but I don't have a favorite team. I always pick the winners. I always root for the team who's going to win. In basketball I like both the NBA and college, and I also like wrestling and tennis and gymnastics.

**Emily:** Did you watch the Olympics?

**Mitchell:** I watched both the Summer and the Winter Olympics. And I like to watch NFL and college football. But my favorite one to watch is the cheerleaders.

I like Syracuse playing college basketball and college football, because they are a good team. Since I live in South Orange and Seton Hall is a college most people go to, me and my father have a rivalry between who's going to win, Seton Hall or Syracuse. Me and my father go to the games and root for our teams. Sometimes we make bets who's going to win and who's not. Syracuse is the college my father went to.

The other rivalry I have is with Gail about the Jets. I always tease her when the Jets lose a game. Gail Ferguson, she's one of the secretaries who works at Colonial Terrace. She's a friend. We usually bet for ice cream. This year I bet for a dinner. And I usually win. Most of the time.

**Jason:** The funny thing about the Yankees and me predicting who's going to win — when the Yanks are losing at the eighth inning, I start rooting for the opposite team to win.

My uncle did read the box scores when we went to the Yankee Stadium for my birthday. He showed me how to read the box scores. I follow whoever wins.

I follow with my dad to be your own pitcher. Before the pitcher really pitches a ball or strike, Dad says you be the umpire. What is this play? I follow the signs: one strike or one ball. At a real game, I see the pitcher pitch the ball and before the batter hits the ball I try to figure whether it's a ball or a strike before the hitter hits the ball.

**Mitchell:** For my birthday, my eighteenth birthday, my father got tickets to Wrestlemania, which was in Atlantic City. So me and my father and Seth Greenberg and his father went to Atlantic City to watch wrestling and we had lots of fun. It's fun seeing them hit each other, throw chairs at each other, it's fun. I have a lot of favorite wrestlers: Ultimate Warrior, Macho Man, Randy Savage.

**Jason:** I've met Larry Holmes. And I saw Sergeant Slaughter. Larry Holmes played my cabbie in the show "Fall Guy." Boxing is okay, but what I don't like is it's too boring than wrestling. I mean — hit with the left, hit with the right and upper cut. It's a little boring than wrestling. Wrestling has headlocks, and diving and kicking.

**Mitchell:** I don't like boxing as much myself, but I do like wrestling because it's a lot of fun to watch it and to see it. Once I remember when we went to the Greenbergs, me, Dad, Seth, and Harry sometimes wrestle with each other. Sometimes the mothers get a little protective because they don't want us to get hurt. Oh, those protective mothers.

**Jason:** That's the difference between fathers and mothers. Fathers get away with it, and mothers overprotective.

**Mitchell:** When I was Bar Mitzvahed, Norman and Diane and Rosanne and Steve took me in a hot-air balloon. It was in Newport, Rhode Island, and . . . we went on it and we went way up in the sky over a thousand feet. It was very beautiful and very fun adventure.

The other fun thing that I've done was I went to a lot of amusement parks. I'm definitely a maniac when it comes to roller coasters. I love roller coasters a lot and I go on those a lot of times. Once I remember that I went on a stand-up roller coaster and I stand up the whole ride.

I went to amusement parks in Canada, in California, in Florida, and around here. The scarier the rides are, the more fun. When I do go to amusement parks, I do go on rides that has double loops or triple loops and I don't get scared because I'm confident most of the time. The important one that I love is the Spider. It goes up around, up and down, upside down. And bumper cars, I like. It's fun doing those. And water parks. I definitely love water slides, water parks.

Once my father and I went to Action Park. I don't remember the name of the ride, but there was a rock way up here and you dive off twenty-five feet into the water. It was twenty-five feet and I did a belly flop on my chest. My father did the same thing. He wasn't going to do it. But because I did a belly flop, then my father dove in to see if I was all right.

I'm usually a good diver. But that one was twenty-five feet.

**Jason:** If I gave you a hint would you guess this ride? Whatever you do, don't blow bubble gum, or whatever you do, don't vomit on this ride. It will come back to you. It comes around and around, and you are stuck in the middle. You can't move around.

**Mitchell:** Oh I love that ride!

**Jason:** . . . It's called the Roundup.

In Wet 'n' Wild in Florida, it was a scary moment of one of the slides. They thought I was stuck in the tube. But I weren't. I got out the bottom okay. But I saw the manager looked above and the man looked below, and they were looking for me. They thought I was stuck in the tube. And I was worried *my parents* were stuck. They were calling into the tube to see if I'm okay. And I were fine. I was at the bottom and I was scared if my mom and dad was stuck in the tube.

There's another ride in Wet 'n' Wild which is every five minutes the machine that makes big waves. You sit in a tube and you wait until the machine starts to do the waves. It was big waves and it was fun. I was scared at first because I thought it was the salty ocean, but it wasn't. It was fresh water.

**Mitchell:** . . . The other thing which I've done with my father is that one time me and my father went white-water rafting. When we were doing the white-water rafting, we went out of the raft and we bodysurfed. It was in Pennsylvania.

I've done bodysurfing. Whenever we go on a family trip, we always go bodysurfing into the waves. My father taught me and my two sisters how to do it, which was lots of fun. When I went to Long Beach Island, I did bodysurfing myself and I enjoyed bodysurfing because it's a lot of fun. It's a grip of life.

I bodysurfed in Hawaii and California. A lot of trips which I went to, I bodysurfed.

**Jason:** In Montauk with Grandpa, we went to fish a lot and I got three snappers. I got about ten snappers when my family came to Sag Harbor. I like going fishing with Gramps. Also near Gedney Park I caught ten sunnies.

I learned how to fish. Worming, baiting, and all that stuff. How I feel about the worms is gooey and that's it.

An old family custom we have is to kiss one of those fish, the first fish [of the season], and throw him back in the water. And I did it. It felt blubbery.

**Mitchell:** . . . Once when we were in Puerto Rico, me and [my sister] Stephanie and my father went on Jet Skis. At first me and Stephanie went on first. Then my father and me went on it. My father was on it and my father fell off and I continued by myself and [that] was very reckless.

**Jason:** I tried the Jet Skis in Cancún. A little two-seater power-boat. Mom did most of the driving up toward the snorkeling place but I did 80 percent of the driving the boat the other way back to the lodge. It felt great. I went fast, faster than anything in the world. It was faster than a DeLorean.

# 7

## Girls and Sex

### "The Tummy Is Sexy
### and the Shoulder Is Friendly"

*July '90*

**Jason:** I got some problems with girls. In school. Like in the halls and waiting for my bus.... [Once] I did something inappropriate like I came up to a girl and said, "Take off your shirt. Let's go out somewhere." She said, "Stop it." I realize it was inappropriate. Now I changed and I am appropriate with girls in school.

Sometimes it's very embarrassing when girls see me when I am blue. Down in the dumps. They think I'm normal. I don't feel normal myself. Normal means how you look and how well you behave. I don't feel I look normal. Sometimes I see my legs and my arms having hair, and I have to start to shave my mustache and beard....

*August '90*

**Jason:** My psychologist thinks that something has to be done with girls that he can try to deal with. There's some girls trying to be nice to me and to inform me about what they expect me into that school.... These girls were trying to keep me out of trouble because I got some severe problems with girls, not exactly inappropriate things, but seeing them what they look like and staring at them. So it's a better idea to keep it for yourself.

Mr. Blitstein is my psychologist. Mr. [Sheldon] Blitstein is the name who helps me a lot to cope with other people and to deal with girls. I see him every once a week on Monday. I talk about some problems with girls that can't be solved until I finish talking. He is trying to prevent me with some girls that can be nicer and can understand me better. He wants me to understand better that being with girls is a big idea, to get out of the situation.

**Mitchell:** On some occasions I was seeing [my psychologist] Vito [Guarnaccia] and when I get together with him, I was talking to him about my problems, problems dealing with school that deal with other students . . . and that I could talk to him. I'd be hearing what the other students were saying. I was seeing Vito once a week, and I'll tell him every week what happened the week in school. He helped me by understanding how to deal with the situation and how to handle it. He also told me what is the better decision than to do the wrong decision.

He would give me some advice, what to do about my problems when I'm in school.

One time when I was in eighth grade, there was one girl in my class by the name of Sherry. Sometime me and her had a small argument and on one occasion, I touched her and I was punished because I did that. I was suspended for a day. Out of school for that.

I wasn't attracted to her at all. We were just friends. I just did it for the fun of it, to get attention. This was in the cafeteria. There were other kids around. Other kids saw me do this. In my relationship with Sherry had a twist to it. Things kind of got changed. Me and Sherry didn't get along at all after that. Afterwards I would make fun of her, laugh at her and do all these inappropriate things.

I was caught and other people were doing the same things to her. I was calling her fat and all these names, like mean names. She probably felt upset and very angry and it meant that she had to talk to someone, which she did. She didn't confront me at all....

I apologized to her, I told her I was sorry. Bob Weston is a psychologist at the school. That once in a while I would see him and we would talk about my problems. After the advice I would stay away from her for a while and that helped. A lot.

Now Sherry's one of my friends. Now I get along with her. I basically talk to her and have some conversations. My behavior is better and improved. I like her *as a friend, just a friend*. I feel embarrassed sometimes when I talk about some of these issues, about the past. And how it was.

*January '91*

**Jason:** Scientific method. Number one: State problem! *Touching girls.*

**Mitchell:** I think I heard this before. Jason, I think you should be very serious about this issue instead of kidding around or laughing.

**Jason:** I know this is serious—but I like what you said.

**Mitchell:** Can you give me some background? How did this problem start out?

**Jason:** When I was looking out for my bus, toward the end of the day in school, I touched a girl, I hugged a girl.

You don't know how hard it is to be a man, and to be independent is what a man can do—or a lady, if a girl wants to be—but you see that person is struggling. That means it's hard to be a man.

**Mitchell:** [*To Emily*] When you spoke to the dean, can you tell me yourself what he told you?

**Emily:** He told me pretty much what Jason said. That Jason had approached a girl in the hall and asked if he could hug her. The girl said no.

**Jason:** In a nonsexual way. Not as boyfriend and girlfriend but just as friends.

**Emily:** But you wanted to know if you could look down her shirt. And she said no. Right?

**Jason:** Right.

**Emily:** That's not just "as a friend." Is it?

**Jason:** No, I guess it's not.

**Emily:** So the dean told me that this happened and the girl wasn't very happy about it. She likes Jason, but not in that way.

**Mitchell:** Was this girl in special ed or in mainstream?

**Jason:** . . . She was in mainstream. It's very different from in special ed. . . . It's very hard for a special ed person to approach a mainstream person like this. I'm glad you came up to that. I didn't realize she was a mainstream girl.

**Mitchell:** Now I'm going to give you my advice to you. How to approach a girl. No matter if mainstream or special ed. Because the way I see a girl, no matter the girl looks like or what, she has to be treated like other people, as same, no matter same or different. Women are most vulnerable at a position. . . .

**Jason:** You mean—that I should treat more respect to other people. To approach a girl, you have to treat her nicely, as friends, not as sexual stuff, no matter if she is mainstream or not, compared to us.

**Mitchell:** That's correct, what you just said. Women like to be treated important. . . . I feel it is inappropriate to go up to a woman and ask if you can hug her. To me that's inappropriate behavior. If you want to ask someone to hug you, outside of school that's okay, but inside school that creates problems. That creates peer pressure. Because with peer pressure, there are lots of people who will try to intimidate you to go out and do something that is wrong. But you know in your heart that it's wrong.

Try to think. What is the important thing? To be in school, to go into classes and have appropriate behavior. That will give you so you won't have a reputation of sexualizing with other women.

**Jason:** I'll keep it in thought and see how I do from that time on.

**Mitchell:** There are certain ground rules you have to face. One of them I have to elaborate on is that no one likes to be sexually harassed.

**Emily:** Mitchell, how do you come to know so much about this topic?

**Mitchell:** Can you rephrase the question?

**Emily:** I know that you are about three years older than Jason. You have had more experience in these matters than he has. So you are in a position to give him good advice. Does this advice come from your own experience in high school?

**Mitchell:** From what I remember, yes, all this does have to reflect my own experience. I started in the ninth grade being a freshman.

I learned to be mature by talking about my problems with certain people in our school. Not basically my friends. Basically teachers or the dean, which I have a good friendship with. They have understanding of what goes around the school building.

**Barbara:** When you were in ninth grade and you thought it was appropriate behavior to put your arms around some of the girls who were your sisters' friends, how did that go over?

**Mitchell:** If I could remember exactly, my two sisters felt uncomfortable that I was harassing their friends. But now up to this date I reflect on that time, and I thought it would be better if I be honest instead of keeping as a secret or lie to other people. But I will elaborate on that. Now I do feel mature and it's time that I change that time into this period of time, a new phase.

**Barbara:** Jason is in ninth grade now. What he was doing with girls is not that much different from what you were doing with girls at that age.

**Mitchell:** That's a little bit different. The way it was different

was that in both my and Jason's mind, we see things differently. When I was in ninth grade, I thought that I knew I was mature and ready for a relationship. I was ready to ask a woman
to go out on dates. But I was a little bit immature about it,
harassing women in school. Eventually I got punished. Like in-
school study center. In other words called in-school suspen-
sion. That is when a student stays in a room with a teacher
who will get the work from the teachers to bring down to the
room to do in there. Because no socializing or anything. Basically very boring.

**Barbara:** Jason, when you were approaching the girl, when
you asked her those questions, do you know why you did it?
Were you curious? Did you like the girl?

**Jason:** I found the girl attractive. She was so pretty. Made me
say those things. But I was a generous person. I shouldn't have
to say those things in the first place. When she says no to me,
that's it. That's final. I'll just stop immediately before I get into
trouble. What I'm going to do. When I approach a girl like this,
I'll say to myself immediately, "Stop, danger, caution, trouble,
touch trouble."

**Mitchell:** What you're saying, what we have to discover is
your motivation. Why you decide to do this. Can you say why
did you do this if you did not expect to get a response back?
How did she react when you did what you did to her?

**Jason:** She reacted embarrassed. She had to respond no.

**Mitchell:** What were the exact words?

**Jason:** She said, "No, you can't do that. Stop it right now."
Then I said, "Okay, you got me there. Bye-bye."

**Barbara:** Is there some kind of strategy that you can use to
make sure you don't approach a girl that way? Some kind of
control?

**Mitchell:** Yes. I'll tell you the exact way. If you go up to a
woman and say, "How you doing," or tell them how beautiful
they look, that would make more attractation, attraction. And

more obvious that they'd be interested in seeing each other. Instead of going up to them and give them a big hug right away. You could say that if she wants to have dinner with you — or go to a movie — to get to know each other better.

**Emily:** Mitchell, have you had the experience of going up to a mainstream girl and asking her if she wants to have dinner with you or go to a movie with you?

**Mitchell:** Yes, I did once. I was rejected. Not because of the disability or anything. Because she was seeing somebody else. This all goes back to the problem, Jason, because probably the girl that you touched was probably seeing somebody else. It's okay to be friends and to socialize, but it's not okay to go up to a woman and expect everything that you want.

Sometimes you have to set your priorities, what is important. The important thing is, Jason, is that if you want to know her, all you have to do is be nice to her and talk to her and get to know her. Then you'll have a better way, a better sense of what's in common to do things together. I know that the guys in school, basically rumors . . . they'd probably talk behind your back, a generalization about you in school. It's not cool doing that. But eventually what's cool about doing that is having a sense of your friends and how they feel and what they say about it.

**Jason:** I might do that for the future. I could go up to a girl and say, "Hi. How are you, what's your name? Maybe when we get older we could have a date together. A weekend."

**Mitchell:** I don't think a woman wants to be asked if you want to spend a weekend. You'd be better off asking her to a movie, not a weekend. It would be better if you get to know her first.

**Jason:** I might have to say, "What's school like? What are your studies? What do you think about me? What do you think can be changed in our lives? How are you getting along with your boyfriend?" Or something.

**Mitchell:** Be serious.

**Jason:** Okay, I'll be serious. "Where have you been all your life?"

**Jason:** I have a relationship with Tami. Tami lives in Pittsburgh, Pennsylvania, far away from here. I take an airplane to see her. Tami is a nice-looking girl, nice curly blond hair, eyeglasses, same religion and without a disability. Tami has Down syndrome but with no disability.

**Mitchell:** Do you feel having a girl closer to you, would that change your feelings for Tami?

**Jason:** It would not change my feelings for Tami in the world. You can live with only one true love, who you are going to get married with. But if you have a semi-girlfriend, which means that you need someone to warm your heart and make you feel special... it's happy and good all over and have being normal.

**Mitchell:** You don't feel different if you have someone in Pittsburgh and someone else close to you? Can you pinpoint... your feelings for Tami? Do you feel the one nearer to you is more important than Tami, yes or no?

**Jason:** No. Tami—because she is my own true love who I have deeply inside my heart. You're looking at a Jason that can be caring to only his love, to get married with, and that's the only girl I'll get married with. But I can still go on dates with other people beside Tami.

**Emily:** Would Tami be jealous?

**Jason:** Not exactly, because she is my true love to get married with.

**Mitchell:** What will Tami think if you do that? How would Tami feel?

**Jason:** She doesn't mind. Unless there's sexual stuff. That makes her jealous. But she'll have to share her sexual stuff with only her and me. I may interact some girls who are pretty, but that doesn't make me change my feelings about Tami. Because I still love Tami a lot.

**Emily:** How about if you heard that Tami was doing sexual stuff with other guys?

**Jason:** I would be upset. I would break up with her and get another girlfriend.

**Mitchell:** I know how it feels, finding the first woman that is important to you, but true love doesn't always come true. I know that from watching shows and experience-wise. Not every person will think the same way. They will feel more important and dignified if a guy like you, Jason, finds someone away from home, that is more difficult to get to. Makes its own problems. You don't know what that girl is doing with other guys. But how are you going to develop a relationship with other women if you are committed to one?

*June '92*

**Mitchell:** I want to enter a relationship with a woman who does not have a disability because that's one of my advantages...because I feel that it's much more appropriate toward my feelings.... I feel that to me, I want to do things with other people in any situation that comes up. And I feel that if I enter a relationship with someone who does not have a disability, it would be better for me.

...A girl with a disability would be more slower and I will not be more understanding of her needs.

I want to be in a relationship that could be more committed and to be in one of those tracks that other people have, that other people are involved in instead of worrying about Down syndrome.

"Hey, I have a disability; I have Down syndrome," and they will understand. Today when I went back to my old high school and the girls came up to me and said, "You were great on the TV show. Hey, I want to be in a relationship with you."

**Jack:** You wanted them to say that! Did they *really* say that?

**Mitchell:** Well, no.

**Jack:** You're saying you don't want to have a romantic relationship with someone with a disability because she might be slower in understanding you and things in life.

But if you're disabled and the woman isn't, then *you're* going to be the one who's slower in understanding than she is. Whereas if you were *both* disabled, you might be able to grow together and learn together.

**Mitchell:** I don't want that. To me it would ruin my reputation. Now people know me who I really am.... Newspapers, TV, and magazines are part of my reputation. Of being a ladies' man.

**Charles:** Do you think a girl would be lucky to get you?

**Mitchell:** A girl without a disability, yes. A girl with a disability would be lucky, too, but I would turn her down.

**Charles:** You find yourself attractive even though you have a disability.

**Mitchell:** Yes.

**Charles:** Sometimes the disability is the attractive part because you've risen above the disability. Couldn't a girl be just as attractive because she rose above *her* disability?

**Mitchell:** Yes, from the perspective of a guy with a disability, I'd say yes. But I can say she would be attractive to Corky [from "Life Goes On"] but not to me because I'd be different.

We're talking about two different backgrounds, two different experiences. What I'm saying is not among the qualities of the common disability.... I'm talking about something different.

What's different is that person's feelings or emotions may be different. To me that I feel that I would feel more attractive to someone who does not have a disability because I feel that I have a lot of things going for me now and I feel that more of myself.

**Jack:** You have to be honest with yourself. You should look for someone who is comparable to you. You get along with Jason because you are comparable with Jason. The same with

# Mitchell

*This was when I was very young,
laying on the bed, playing around.*

*This was taken when I was on
the back porch, playing on a climber.*

*This is a picture of myself at school.*

*This was when I was on the beach
going swimming.*

## Mitchell

*Me and my two sisters, Stephanie and Leah, when we were at Camp Mill Run.*

*Me and my two parents rehearsing for my Bar Mitzvah.*

*This picture was taken when I was playing soccer.*

This picture was taken at my sister Leah's Bat Mitzvah.

My two grandparents, Lee and George Gibbs, and myself at a restaurant having a birthday dinner together.

Me and State Assemblyman George Pataki in Albany, where he introduced me to the Assembly.

MITCHELL: *This picture was taken during Halloween, when I was dressed up as a chef.*

JASON: *This is me in Halloween when I was dressed up as a clown holding a pumpkin. It was taken at nursery school when I was three years old.*

# Mitchell and Jason

MITCHELL: *This was taken at my house at a birthday party for one of my sisters. We were sitting down, enjoying our company.*  JASON: *I think Mitchell was so cute and the girls were very pretty.*

JASON: *This was taken at the Colonial Terrace at the reception after the Bar Mitzvah. I felt very glad that Mitchell was being Bar Mitzvahed. I am very proud of him.*

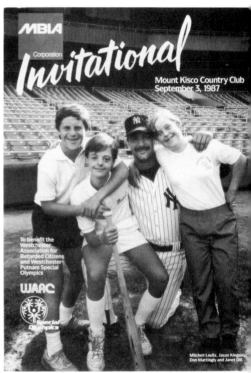

## Mitchell and Jason

JASON: *This picture was taken at Yankee Stadium with Don Mattingly for the cover of the MBIA Invitational journal. Our friend Janet Dill was part of it.*

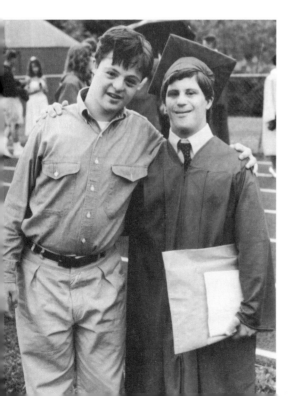

MITCHELL: *This was taken in June '91 when I graduated from high school. I received my diploma and several awards. My friend Jason was there to wish me good luck.*

# Jason

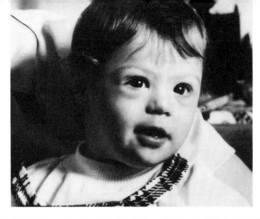

*This is me when I was young, about one year old. I am very cute. It was taken at Finmor Drive, my old house.*

*This is on "Sesame Street," when the Cookie Monster was showing everyone that I knew how to read.*

*In 1980, me and my brother Glenn went to Todd's graduation. Todd had put his graduation hat on my head.*

*This is me with Governor Cuomo. He was a guest speaker and I was a guest of honor at a black-tie dinner for Special Olympics.*

*This is me with my love, Tami. She lights up my life.*

## Jason

*This is me with my grandpa going fishing at Gedney Park. . . . Grandpa is my favorite and best grandpa of all times. He feels like the same kid I do.*

In 1990 our family went to see Rose Kennedy's
100th birthday and receive a Kennedy award
by Ethel Kennedy. We were happy and honored.

# Jason

My hobby is making oil paintings of landscapes.
This is one of my best favorites.

In 1992, this is me voting for the
presidential elections. I voted for
the winner, Mr. Clinton. This is the
first time I voted in any election.

your roommate Ted. You have to be honest with yourself and realize that girls like yourself will be better for you.

**Mitchell:** Charles, I was wondering as a father of Jason, I'm interested in your perspective and opinion of Jason and Tami's relationship.

**Charles:** Think you can handle it?

**Mitchell:** Yes.

**Charles:** Well, at one time Jason was madly in love with a girl named Leah. Yes, your sister. That scared the hell out of me. One of the happiest moments of my life was when he fell in love with Tami instead of Leah. Can you understand why?

**Mitchell:** It's not just because we knew each other. Tell me if I'm right or wrong. You feel protective of Jason because you may not be so sure that my sister would be the right one for him, because of her feelings and his feelings. I don't know the right word for it.

**Charles:** You're somewhat on track, but I'm not sure if you're exactly on track. My feeling was that Leah would eventually go on to college and would become a doctor or a lawyer or something. She would always feel deeply for Jason. But eventually, she would leave Jason behind—because she grew past him—and that would give me a lot of pain.

Now with Tami, or another girl who has similar skills, similar potential to Jason, they could grow together. And develop comfort with each other and love for each other and safety with each other.

Mitchell, you have a bias and a prejudice against a girl with a disability. You don't want a girl with a disability.

**Mitchell:** There are a lot of interpretations of being prejudiced.

**Charles:** If you can't consider a girl with a disability, that's a prejudice.

**Jack:** You're not even giving yourself a chance. Why does the title of "girlfriend" make such a difference? Why can't the same girl who is your friend also be a girlfriend? Why couldn't you kiss her?

**Mitchell:** Because I feel insecure. I feel they're more slower. It's quite embarrassing to me, outside. They're too slow.... If it was kept inside the building, then fine.

**Jack:** Even someone like Erica's too slow?! At what? Erica can run rings around you!

**Mitchell:** She's slow in expressing how she feels.

**Jack:** That might be good news, not bad news.

**Charles:** How about Andrea Friedman, the girl with Down syndrome on "Life Goes On"? She's terrific. She's pretty and she drives a car and she goes to college and everything. Seems to me Andrea Friedman would be the catch of a lifetime.

**Mitchell:** For Jason, yes, not for me.

### September '92

**Jason:** There was a dance and I met Tracy Fields. She is twelve years old. She is blushing. Is tall and beautiful and a blond girl. She has very long legs. She wore a nice cutoff back-off green dress with a low neckline. I thought I was being nervous or having a dream.

She took my hand and sat down for a while and had a drink (a Coke) and when it's time for her to go home, Tracy and I made a two-minute kiss. She had her mouth inside of my mouth. She began to kiss me and I kissed her back. And she didn't have any Down syndrome.

She is so blushing modest, so gorgeous. She's a pretty young girl.

It was too confusing if Tami was there. Because Tami might think that she might be jealous going out to another girl. And she would have been broken up with me. If she saw me kissing Tracy. But I really enjoyed it.

Tracy lives in Oklahoma. I thought she was living in Philadelphia, but she gave me her address and she lives in

Oklahoma. I would like to see her again. I hope we'll keep in touch. I can't wait to get a four-week vacation with her.

**Emily:** What would you do?

**Jason:** Kiss a lot.

**Emily:** For four weeks?!

**Jason:** Yeah!

*August '90*

**Emily:** When we're talking about sex, having sex with someone, what does that mean to you?

**Mitchell:** Sex means to take a commitment, that means a lot for me and the woman.

**Emily:** What physically? Bodywise?

**Mitchell:** I mean it's like being naked, no clothes, the man's penis and the woman's vagina will meet. I mean the egg and the sperm. They'll meet and once they're together it becomes making a baby.

**Jason:** Love 'em. Hug her. And kiss her. And show that you care and respect for her. They're rubbing and waiting for sperm to come out of a man's penis to make a baby.

**Emily:** Can you have sex without making a baby?

**Mitchell:** I don't think so, no.

**Jason:** You might say it's impossible, but I think once you're at home you can think about your girl and that is called a wet dream. Something sticky comes out and you feel as if you have sticky pajamas. It's called a wet dream. You can't make a baby until you see your love and make sex.

**Mitchell:** I think when a person wants to have a child is when you do it, have sexual intercourse. A male and a female make love, they have sexual intercourse, two people making a commitment and doing it. Sometimes they can go a whole night or a whole day.

**Emily:** But the only times you do that is when you want to have a baby?

**Mitchell:** Yes.

**Jason:** I think you can get a baby while making sex ... and sex is too much fun. You can have sexual intercourse with a lady and you can't stop making sex with her.... And you can do it for the whole day, probably the whole night, probably the whole two days, probably the whole month.

**Mitchell:** Seriously, Jason, if you were married and you want to have sex, how are you and Tami going to go about birth control? Sometimes when a woman would take birth control pills, they are thinking about protection, how the baby will grow up.

**Jason:** What if two people want to have sex but don't want to have a baby?

**Mitchell:** If a male and a female already had sex one time and they decide not to have a child, they'll probably decide to put the child up for adoption and give the child up.

**Emily:** When they have as many children as they want, do they stop having sex, making love? Or do they continue?

**Mitchell:** They may continue for the fun of it, not to have another child. Then they use protection.

**Jason:** What I learned in school that Tami and I should not make love because most teenagers don't know about AIDS.

**Mitchell:** During the summer I met this girl by the name of Janette. She lives in Ossining and she's about my age. She has dark hair and she is very attractive. She enjoys sports and she enjoys spending time with me. We always have pleasant conversations. I met her this summer and ... I plan to see her pretty soon.

*October '90*

**Charles:** We were talking about sex. Who is the ideal girl? Do you have an actress or a famous person or somebody in your school or in your class? Who is it you really admire as a girl, and what do you admire most?

**Mitchell:** Well, I'm not going to be naming names, or anything, but I'll say that I want to find a woman who understands me and who has a great personality and looks and everything, but more importantly, how she feels about a person with a disability and how she would react to it. And if she feels comfortable going out with me, I would feel more than glad to take the next step.

**Charles:** Jason, who's your ideal girl? Do you think Tami is beautiful?

**Jason:** Yes, I think Tami is beautiful. If you say comparison like "Who do you like the prettiest?" Tami or Susan Akin* or [my friend] Ada. I think Tami is the prettiest.

**Charles:** Do you think Ada is sexy?

**Jason:** I think Ada is quite sexy, but Tami is more mentally sexy.

**Jack:** What do you mean by that?

**Jason:** Mental kind of way is what you feel of your love.

**Mitchell:** So, Jason, the way you feel about Tami, is it for respect or looks?

**Jason:** Looks.

**Mitchell:** Why do you choose looks over respect? If you know that respect is more important...

**Jack:** Mitchell, do you go for looks, or do you go for respect?

**Mitchell:** I go for respect.

**Jack:** You're full of baloney.

**Mitchell:** Well, seriously, which I know about,... most of the girls in the mainstream go for respect and not for looks.

**Charles:** What makes a girl sexy?

**Mitchell:** Everything.... [But] the sexiest part of a woman is the personality.

I would [also] say their irresistible smile, sparkling eyes, and what's all about her.

**Charles:** What about you, Jason?

---

*Miss America, 1986, who had a sister with Down syndrome

**Jason:** Her insides. Deep inside — like her breast.

**Mitchell:** Let's not get to profanity.... The reason we're doing this book for, it's not for language usage, it's about feelings.

I don't want to name any parts because I just feel like I don't want to say naming parts, because I will feel like if a woman is sexy I will go for it but not naming body parts.

**Charles:** Could you talk to your friends at school about it?

**Mitchell:** They would feel uncomfortable talking to their parents about it.

**Charles:** What about talking to each other?

**Mitchell:** That's something different.

**Charles:** Do you think that sex is just in your head at this point, just a fantasy, or do you really feel interested in sex with girls at this time?

**Mitchell:** What I'm saying is like when I'm talking about women is the way I feel for them, is the way I love them. Not about like talking to my father about it. I feel a little insecure about it. Talking to my father, it's like that would give me the wrong approach and not feel like I would take what I feel would be the best approach for myself.

**Jack:** In other words, you don't want to ask me my advice about women? You figure you know how to deal with it yourself.

**Mitchell:** That's correct.

**Charles:** What about you, Jason? In your case you've touched girls in school — a couple of times last year, a couple of times this year. It's always on the shoulder or the stomach. Is that because you find the shoulders sexy or the stomach sexy, or are you just being friendly?

**Jason:** I think they were shoulders or tummy. I think the tummy is sexy and I found that the shoulder is friendly.

### April '91

**Jason:** Hey Mitchell, you think you should go into a club of naked ladies?

**Mitchell:** I'm a ladies' man. Hey Mom, I got a question for you. Would you go into a club of naked men?

**Barbara:** Definitely not. I'm not interested. I'd be embarrassed.

**Jason:** Mom, would you go to a formal dinner with my father, your husband?

**Emily:** Sure. Why not?

**Jason:** Then take me with you!

**Barbara:** Eventually you guys will find your own women and go to your own formal dinners.

**Mitchell:** Without our mothers there to nag us all the time.

**Emily:** Jason, why did you bring up the club of naked women? Is that where you would like to go?

**Jason:** Well, I do it when the time is ripe.

**Mitchell:** I do it *any* time.

**Barbara:** Oh sure.

*September '92*

**Emily:** Last night we watched "Life Goes On" and it was about AIDS and HIV positive, and you were concerned about you and Tami and whether you could have sex and get HIV and stuff like that.

**Jason:** The reason why I watch that show because I am very protective on the subject of HIV.... I want to make sure that we don't get it. I don't have and neither does her. I want to make sure it stays that way.

The way to make sure that we are protective and have safety. The best way to have safety is no sex. If you do get sex, for protection of AIDS and HIV is you use a condom. I have some on my first right drawer. I hadn't used them yet because I didn't have sex yet. But when I do, I got my condoms with me.

# 8

# Marriage and Children

## "A Together Bed for You and Me"

*August '90*

**Barbara:** What [sort of a woman] are you looking to marry?

**Mitchell:** A woman who is very sweet, very attractive, and a woman who believes in me, who has a personality and understands how I feel.

**Barbara:** What's attractive?

**Mitchell:** A woman who has such beauty, beautiful eyes, beautiful smile, gentle and tender lips with the sparkle, the way she moves, and a woman who can tame this beast.

**Barbara:** Where do you think you might meet someone like this?

**Mitchell:** Somewhere in California. California babes. By going out, hanging out at the beach, by looking at 'em, and by going up to them and saying, "Hey Chickie baby!"

**Barbara:** Do you think the social club you're in [City Lights] can help you meet women you might want to marry someday?

**Mitchell:** Yes in capital letters.

**Barbara:** Do many of the young women in your social club have disabilities?

**Mitchell:** Yes, some do. I have no objections to marrying a woman with a disability, [as long as she has] blond hair and blue eyes. Dark hair is okay.

**Emily:** Who do you want to marry, Jason?

**Jason:** Hot, steamy, and sexy. Means very slim body, nice shine, nice tan, nice cute little face, nice big cute smile, like put suntan lotion on her back and say, "Ooo baby I love ya."

Probably I might take her to a hot steaming restaurant.

**Mitchell:** I'd take her to a hot steaming hot tub.

**Jason:** A hot steaming bubble bath. Like I have to get ready for a nice date together with a restaurant, take a bite somewhere, then swim in the pool. I'll describe what she wears in the pool. A hot-looking bikini. I'm gonna find her in her hotel room. In the Sheraton.

**Jason:** Tami and I are planning to get married. We've talked about it and we both said yes.

**Mitchell:** Jason, do you think you're kind of young to talk about marriage now?

**Jason:** Well, Tami is quite young to do it, but not me 'cause I'm sixteen years old and I could know about the marriage myself. I could learn more about love and what this hot steamy relationship.

I might go out with some other people for a date, but I'll still love Tami more.

**Mitchell:** In the future, if you're not married to Tami, will you have another love interest with another woman?

**Jason:** I'll keeping trying and trying with Tami, 'cause Tami and I said yes. I'll never give up.

**Mitchell:** Is it better to talk to your parents before you have this conversation with Tami?

**Jason:** No, I think my decision is made up, to marry Tami. But I'll still going to go out with other girls.

**Mitchell:** When do you plan to marry Tami?

**Jason:** About five more June 27s. When I'm twenty-one and she'll be twenty.

**Mitchell:** Do you feel your education should come first, then get married to Tami? Or the reverse?

**Jason:** I think I have to worry about Tami first and then back to my education....

**Mitchell:** If your parents decide they want you to finish your education, but you want to marry Tami, what would you do?

**Jason:** I have to explain to my parents how much I love Tami and how much I know her so I can marry her, and once we have children I can go back to my education and to teach my kids when they get older about my job.

In the meantime, it's same as me, I'll still go on dates with other girls and still love Tami, and Tami can go with other boys and wait for me.

**Mitchell:** What if somebody else wants to marry Tami in the meantime?

**Jason:** Then I'll go and fight for her.

**Mitchell:** Would you feel jealous if Tami was seeing another guy?

**Jason:** I *might* be a little bit of jealous, but you wait for me to say okay to see another guy. It's okay to see another guy, but it's not okay to look at the person's body and touch them. I don't want her to have sex with him.

**Mitchell:** Is it okay to have sex with you?

**Jason:** It's better have to sex with me—before and after we're married. Before you're married it's okay to have sex,... and after you're married you can get some more sex until you go to the hospital until Tami feels a baby inside.

**Mitchell:** Would you push her to have sex with you, or would you wait until she feels comfortable?

**Jason:** I think I wait until she feels comfortable. If I push her to have sex, it looks like a one-sided person.... I don't want to have sex with her unless it's okay with both people.

**Mitchell:** I think I would wait until she is ready. I think once I get married to a woman, then I would take a very serious commitment, that the responsibilities, take care of my wife, take care of my children. In my marriage, if a woman that I chose to have sex with, if she agrees and is ready to take the commitment, to take the step in our relationship, then I would be ready and I would have sex with her. Then I would probably decide, if she was taking birth control pills. If she decides to take birth control pills, then I would tell her, don't worry about protection. . . .

**Emily:** Do you want to have children?

**Jason:** Yeah. So I could teach them easy stuff for kids. I could have a lot of toys, handheld soft dolls for the baby. I was thinking of having seven children. I might be assistant coach of the baseball team. Seriously, I think I'll have two or three kids. If four, two boys and two girls.

**Emily:** Would you be disappointed if you didn't have children in your life?

**Jason:** Yes, I will.

**Emily:** Did you and Tami ever talk about that?

**Jason:** Yes, Tami and I was going to a date and at lunchtime and so I told her about it and she said yes.

**Mitchell:** The way I want to live, I want to have a family of my own. Have children. I'm undecided about how many number of children. And get married. I want to live in a house, which I can afford, with the job I'm taking. In this house I'd like to live with my immediate family, not my natural parents—I would say my own family, my wife, my children.

**Barbara:** What if you weren't able to have children?

**Mitchell:** Then I could adopt a child.

**Barbara:** If it were very difficult to adopt, how would you feel?

**Mitchell:** I would not be upset, but I would understand why I can't have a child of my own. If a professional said I couldn't have a child, I would understand, [but] not a person who's on the streets.

**Jason:** It would be such a pain. I would be upset. I really want to have children. I think I would be a good father.

**Barbara:** Do you think you could lead a full life if you didn't have children?

**Mitchell:** Yes, I could lead a full life, yes. Even without children. I would be able to continue with my job and continue on being married and continue on being independent.

**Jason:** . . . I don't think I could lead a full life without children. Like when I do my job, I need some money to support my children and my wife. So they can have better foods they can eat. I can buy some food for the people who are poor and for my family. And I have some children to play with after my job is finished.

*August '91*

*Tami is in town visiting Jason.*

**Emily:** Do you think you two guys are going to be together someday?

**Tami:** Yes!

**Jason:** Yes!

**Tami:** When I'm twenty and he's twenty-two. We can celebrate the Fourth of July on our wedding day.

**Jason:** Independence Day which means we'll be doing our independence skills on July 4th.

**Emily:** Where do you think the two of you will live?

**Jason:** In the apartment halfway between Pittsburgh and Chappaqua. . . . I can call my side of the town, and Tami will call her side of the town. Halfway between so that way I can visit with you and I can visit with them, too. I think I might come home near the afternoon evening, like when Daddy comes home. About six o'clock so I can have six-thirty dinner. Exactly like Dad.

**Tami:** I'm coming home about five-thirty so I can do some work at home. I'll make dinner.

**Jason:** Not you alone.

**Tami:** Both of us.

**Jason:** And here's a problem. If we're trying to get some kids, who will take care of the kids when you and I are out?

**Tami:** The baby-sitter. We will hire a baby-sitter. They'll feed them and take care of them till we get home.

**Jason:** We'll go out to a fancy place with candlelight, wine, and soft music.

**Tami:** And maybe a movie.

**Jason:** And maybe go over to my new job or visit your job. Just like my father goes to see his job. Guess who will be the baby-sitter we will hire? Mom.

**Emily:** Me?

**Tami:** You and my mom.

**Emily:** I would *love* to baby-sit for your kids, but if you live halfway to Pittsburgh, that's too far for me to come to baby-sit. That's about four hours away.

**Jason:** That's all right. Mom would go over to the uptown half, and Tami's mom would go to the downtown half.

**Emily:** How many kids are you planning on having?

**Jason:** Seven.

**Tami:** *Seven?*

**Jason:** When they get older they can sing "Doe a Deer."

**Tami:** Seven is too much. Three is better because Jason['s family] has three people — three brothers — and I have three sisters. Seven is too much.

**Jason:** Four. One uptown boy, one downtown boy. One uptown girl, one downtown girl. [*laughs*]

**Emily:** You'll have to have very good jobs to make enough money to raise four kids. It costs a lot of money to raise children nowadays.

**Jason:** How much money will we need for four children?

**Tami:** A lot.

**Jason:** Can you guess or estimate?

**Tami:** I don't know.

**Emily:** Well, you need a very big apartment with enough bedrooms for you and then those four children.

**Jason:** Three bedrooms. One for the downtown kids, one for the uptown kids, then the family room.

**Tami:** We can have bunk beds.

**Jason:** A together bed for you and me, and separate beds

for the kids. Boys sleep with the boys. Girls sleep with the girls.

**Tami:** One big crazy family.

**Jason:** One crazy family with three family bedrooms.

**Tami:** And two crazy grandparents, and two crazy baby-sitters.

**Jason:** To our apartment we'll have a new name. We'll call it the Crazy Apartment. It will be a happy, laughing place.

**Emily:** Do you think you'll be very happy?

**Tami:** Yes!

**Jason:** Yes . . . it will be a comedy in our apartment but we'll be happy.

**Emily:** Do you want a big wedding?

**Jason:** A very big wedding. I decided to have my part-time job friends, my world friends, the president, the vice-president, Gorbachev and the Middle East people, the African people, Masafumi and Alice, European and Latin American people. All the people in the world will come here. Even Don Mattingly. And Balboni. And Roberto and Pat Kelly. Van Slyck. Drabek.

**Tami:** That's the Pirates' pitcher.

**Jason:** Michael Jordan, M. C. Hammer . . .

**Tami:** . . . Isaiah Thomas . . .

**Jason:** The Detroit Pistons. Mort and Rita [Ross] will do the violins for our wedding.

**Tami:** And Vanilla Ice.

**Jason:** And a big wedding cake. Seven floors up. A big bottom, a middle-size middle, the third medium, the fourth medium, the fifth small, the sixth little, and the seventh tiny. And on top of it is Tami and me.

**Tami:** And no cherries.

**Jason:** No cherries! And no mushrooms!

**Tami:** Four hundred people.

**Jason:** Four thousand!

**Tami:** Okay, four thousand!

**Jason:** You can do five rows of chairs of eight hundred people in each line. No cherries, no mushrooms. "... And two hard-boiled eggs!"

**Mitchell:** ... Jase, it is very highly irregular for a person with Down syndrome to get married. For what I see, that part of my future, is to have my own wife but that's difficult to make a commitment. Because once you actually make that commitment, you have to live with that commitment the rest of your life.

**Jason:** I can't live single all my life!

**Mitchell:** How do you know you'll marry Tami? You can't predict that will happen. But you have to be realistic. What's important to you? Is it marriage—which is highly irregular—or to have a future, or both? Because it works both ways. Because this summer, I've grown up a lot. Other summers I grew up more, but this summer I realized there's more to life than what you think.

**Emily:** Why do you feel it's so highly irregular for you to get married?

**Mitchell:** Because from what I hear and what I see, not a lot of people with disabilities are able to get married. Because it is difficult to make a commitment to a woman and to be able to be a father. Sometimes, when you have sex, it is difficult for a guy with Down syndrome ... to get a woman pregnant.

**Emily:** There's a big difference between being married and being a father. Many people are married who don't have children. Even if you're married you can be happy and married and still not have children.

**Mitchell:** That's true. I'm just saying certain people. Certain people with disabilities. Yesterday on "Donahue" (I'm not sure if you watched that), there was a girl named Suzanne and she was ... physically handicapped. She has no arms. By looking at her and realize that if somebody is physically handicapped they can make a difference in life. Because the important part is that a person is special and has a gift. They can show that gift to the others. A lot of people understand about their emotions and how they will feel about the person who is disabled.

What I'm trying to say is, in general, people with disabilities doesn't get married. But I'm trying to prove to others, including Jason, that I'm able to make that commitment. I'm willing to show the others with disabilities that I can. And that's one of the reasons, in order to be a leader, with my experience, down the road five or ten years, to run for president of the United States.

**Jason:** What I heard that it's easy to make a commitment to get married because, if I can get the skills down pat and reach to the age of getting married, I may decide to get married, or I may live single or something. But if you live single, and the apartment is for mothers, if you have kids, who will expect to have kids without a wife to take care of them? You have to get married. That's a law. I can't get children out of myself. I need a wife if I'm going to have children.

**Mitchell:** If I may integrate what he said, you said about marriage that it's easy to make a commitment. You're saying people, other people without disabilities. You're misleading some information because the information that people need to know, I said before, it is *not* easy for people with disability to make a commitment of marriage.

**Emily:** Why is it harder for people with disabilities to make that commitment?

**Mitchell:** Because people don't understand why marriage is so important. Because it's difficult to understand all of the commitments that you have to make. In perspective, you have to look at the charts and graphs.

How are people with disabilities able to make that commitment if they see other people, people who are normal, are able to make that commitment? Two-way crosswise streets. It's easier for people without disabilities because they have better knowledge and better experience of dating and how to deal and how to face it.

*November '92*

**Jason:** Traditions and beliefs can pass down to the future because it starts with parents. The values of parents get passed to me and that's what's happening now. Now I have lots of great importances, but now I have that same values as my parents, I can teach it to my future kids when I get married to Tami.

Before that, I would like to have traditions with Tami, see if Tami agrees on it for our future and then we could pass the traditions down to our children....

**Emily:** What are the values that you and Tami would pass on to your children?

**Jason:** If I were a parent of my future children, my values would be a little the same as my regular parents which are the grandparents of my future kids. I would teach them all the things happening today. Especially some holidays we can pass down like Hanukkah and Passover if the kids are born Jewish. I would teach the kids what my regular parents did to me... which is read, count, ... and important stuff like schools and future.

**Mitchell:** Parents from my perspective give their children, teach them a lot about family values. One of the important values they give to the children is about love, commitment, responsibility, and how important you are to others. It is really about how much you care, how much important your values are to an individual.

It would be too premature that I will be married or have my own children. It's too premature to get into. But we should stick to the basics by establishing what are family values and why are they important.

Going through the family history, you can look at how family values become an individual. The reason of that concept, if you look at it, every grandfather, every grandparent, and every parent will discover lots of new different values, and those values are taught by the parents or grandparents to the child because they want the best kind of life for their child. It is really about how much love and compassion that you have. That's what really counts about values.

. . . You're saying about you and Tami about building a family because I know it is a very different step of doing that. It takes experience. I know I don't have that kind of experience myself. I know it is best that you have this discussion with your parents. They'll give you better advice about this matter instead of assuming you'll have a family of your own.

**Jason:** I do have a lot of experience of dating Tami, and if I'm okay of dating Tami or any other people for now, then I'll make the assumption of deciding I want to get married to Tami. That's the beginning of marriage is deciding after experience.

I'm developing a relationship with Ellen, Janet, somehow Kimberly, and "the famous Tracy Fields." I pretty much know a couple of those experiences that I can do in the future with Tami. I can still develop more. Because I like to do some more dates. But I don't do dates every day because I go to school far away and I'm lacking in social, which [my psychologist] Vito [Guarnaccia] is helping me with . . . like calling people on the phone.

And that's part of the big problem to fix that, because I want to have more social experience with dating. Getting together with boys is okay as friends. But girls, getting to know them, I'd be happy to do it.

. . . But I would like to keep my experience up by dating again and now I'm making decisions of what my values are and what kind of things and responsibilities for me to do in the future of marrying Tami. It's premature but it's okay . . . after you have the experience to decide if you want to get married.

**Mitchell:** Did you see "Life Goes On" last week when Corky and Amanda got married? This really falls into the category with you and Tami because you're saying you'll get married to Tami no matter what.

It's the same situation with Corky and Amanda. Last week they went behind their parents' back and they got the marriage license and the papers in order to get married, which they did last week on that episode. But eventually I felt they were too young to get married because it is a premature decision. They needed to consult with the parents first about to get married or not.

It is a certain concept of understanding about commitment. They've been in love, dating and stuff like that, like you and Tami have been doing,... but there is a different concept. I don't think you understand about commitment.

You take on every responsibility of what kind of loving husband can you be for your wife. There's two ways of looking at this. When I look at you, I think of the kind of friendship that we have. I feel that it is too premature to state in your mind that you want to get married now. You are too young to be married or to assume in the future that you will get married. I think what you said about dating other people is the right thing instead of getting married to one person.

**Jason:** I'm saying I want to keep my dating for right now and probably I can decide I can marry to Tami but still go on dates. When time goes on, and into the future, then I can do it. I have my marriage cold in my mind into the future. If I'm twenty-two and she's twenty-one, I'll think about getting married. That's legal. I'm saying I'll keep dating until I'm twenty-two or older.

**Mitchell:** But then there's something you forgot. Can you commit yourself of doing one thing and the other? That is a big step, a big responsibility. You have to think about it before you state it cold in your mind.

There is other things, other ways of looking at this. One is to be open-minded, listening to what other people say. Two, you can have your perspective as well. The third step is about learning about it, about commitment, or the other stuff.

If you look at it, about building a relationship, you said you wanted to date more. What happens if you get close to another woman? And then you're deeply in love with her and you feel the same way as you do with Tami. That would cause a conflict. The conflict is not going to be happy for you. That would put you in a difficult situation that would be difficult to get out of.

That's why you have to consult with your parents. Certain things you can handle yourself and certain things you cannot. From my perspective, you may disagree, your parents know much more about it because they understand both perspectives and both understandings. That's why I cannot support your decision to get married to Tami at this time.

**Jason:** I would like to move on to other different things. I can be responsible for my own needs. If I'm stuck on something, I can talk to my parents, but I can get out of this conflict myself and move on to something else.

I don't need my parents. All I have to do is still keep my relationship with Tracy but be with her when I go to Oklahoma and evaluate my girls and so I can date with my own true love, which is Tami when she comes in town.

**Barbara:** What does it take to be ready to get married?

**Jason:** You need to be able to make judgments and to be more independent as possible, only for yourself alone or with somebody you're close with. And you can start to do that for a couple of years, three or four years, until you decide if you want to be engaged at first.

Engaged is a big step. We know that. In "Life Goes On," the last couple of weeks, I saw about Amanda and Corky they are doing independence and without the parents along. They can get more deeply involved with independence and for the next issue of "Life Goes On," Corky might have a meeting with

Amanda that it's not going very well but we can do more by learning more things. Easy steps. What I call it "baby steps." If Amanda agrees on it, then they can move on to do more independent things.

I think they're still a little bit on the deciding part. If Corky decides on getting married to Amanda, it can be a different perception for the people who are watching "Life Goes On." Decision-making is close to actual doing it.

Right now they are all finished with their thinking. They think they are getting married. They are planning and that's where independence comes to get married. If you take one of these independence skills, it can be a big step in their future.

**Mitchell:** To me it has to do with — can you do it or not? It is really about how you really feel.

If you really feel you want to get married, you should consult with your parents about the decision so that they could help you to decide to make a better decision, instead of... jumping into it and getting married without consulting. To me in common sense, I would consult with my parents first before making the decision. I could listen to their advice about what I should do.

If I felt I wanted to get married, I would tell the person I'm in love with the way I feel about my feelings. Feelings can be very intimate a lot of times. I would say that it takes time to understand that you need to think about it before doing it.

**Charles:** If you got married today, do you see certain problems you would have?

**Mitchell:** It is really too premature to state if you are ready. I don't have the experience. To be a good husband, you need to be able to understand how important and how are you going to support yourself and your wife. It takes a lot of time to understand all different kind of skills. It takes months and months to learn different kinds of skills.

To take myself as an example, I've been living in South Orange over a year, developing skills to live independently in the future. Part of my future plans is to marry and have a wife, but I need more skills.

Being in a program and asking for help to learn other skills. For example, how to be a good loving husband, how to support yourself financially. And how to support your wife. Part of it that you have to learn is that how are you going to respond to people and how to respond to people around you who might say, "You're married? How about your disability?"

Because of that effect it would be harder for persons like myself to understand the word *commitment*. In order to have a commitment and to be married, you have to understand problems are going to occur and lots can happen. I can state some examples: how to support yourself [and] where are you going to live. All that takes time and you have to work out the planning. Where you're going to get the money from.

All different kinds of things are part of this, and it takes a long time and having a job. If you have a job then you can support yourself and your wife.

**Jason:** I'm in the stage right now of having a job. I volunteer at the Chappaqua Library. In a couple of months they might give me a paying job. Four dollars and sixty-five cents to start.

**Barbara:** What kinds of skills would you need to be a good husband?

**Jason:** To be a good husband is having fun together. What fun means to me is probably you can keep an apartment and keep a job—but what you say about a job is a little different. How about a full-time career? It's true a career is a job of course, but a career is a big step.

Like I would be happy to go to a school and have a career as a teacher's aide, which is a career which I can plan to get money. And then what Dad said about can I support Tami is I can really support her lovingly, romantically, and the next step is independently. Doing skills, independence skills, with her. In your apartment, the skills that you need is the independence skills that you need, like doing laundry and hanging clothes up, ironing, life skills, your own schedule of your transportation.

I have to help Tami, and Tami has to help me. The emotional part of it is that you can feel warmhearted, lovingly, and to keep yourself going with your wife. If you are disabled, you can do it or you can learn.

**Mitchell:** If you're disabled has some effect. That is very difficult. I'm living in a program learning new skills in order to be fully independent. How well can you commit yourself to develop new skills on your own without relying on anybody.

I've been in Jespy over one year and I've been able to do lots of things I've never done before. For example, I never cooked before, and that I'm doing now on my own without any help. There are a lot of things people need to work on and it takes time. The main thing is if you want to get married, you need to have these skills to be developed in order to have a marriage. In order to have a marriage, you have to love each other, you need to understand how you both feel about each other emotionally and about support. Because there are two ways of supporting. You can support yourself and have your own job, and your wife will do the same thing. She'll have her own job and her own life as well. What doesn't go away is how much they care about each other, and that is what counts. How much you love each other and want to commit to each other and stay in the relationship.

**Jason:** About Tami and I, I always love her even though I have some troubles. Emotionally we can all feel warmhearted and it's easy. We can feel supporting is easy because you're thinking about you and your future. But there is a lot of things to learn—but to deal with it is what you said about loving each other. We got that pretty good.

**Mitchell:** There's one thing about you and Tami you should know. I think that you have a long way to go in developing these kinds of skills, and so do I. I have a long way to go to build skills on a relationship, too. I don't have those kinds of skills. I don't have the same kind of socializing.

You have been dating, but I haven't. I have a very good friend of mine.... She has been having a lot of problems. I've been there for her. I gave her my perspective and she respected that. I help her a lot. I do understand how important that you love Tami a lot, but I do think you have a long way to go to a commitment.

**Jason:** Now I'm old enough to decide what commitments to make and what are good commitments and what are bad commitments, to know what they are. To wrap this section up is, I can do your method, what you said earlier, but I want you to keep in mind that I am ready to talk about it. I am now deciding, but I rather talk about it and do things with Tami. Do you think that I'm old enough to decide and talk about the commitments I need?

**Mitchell:** I think it is wise for you to talk about it and have a discussion about it, but I do not think you should go ahead and do it. As I said before, taking time to handle these skills, you should rely on your parents because your parents can understand where you're coming from because they understand you and want to help you.

It is based on trust and honesty. It is about that. It is about opening up. About talking, letting your feelings come out about the way you really feel. That's what you should do. Take things slowly so they can help you to develop the kind of relationship you want instead of doing things on your own. Developing priorities. I think you should have a discussion first instead of making a decision on your own.

**Jason:** I like to make a decision on my own. I'll think about it first. I can talk to myself first.

**Mitchell:** It's up to you and your parents what you want to do. I'm trying to give you my honest opinion. I do think you need to work on this a little more and have a discussion on this before you go ahead and make a decision on your own. I do think you should consult with your parents.

**Jason:** You're talking about parents. I'm talking about individual decisions.

# 9
# Important People
# in Our Lives

## "The Kind of Person I'd Like to Be"

*November '92*

*The following is a conversation between Mitchell and his grandfather George Gibbs.*

**Grandpa:** I have to say to you that one of the happiest days of my life was the day you were born. I felt so excited and so exhilarated to have a grandson that it really meant an awful lot to me. And since that time, we have had such a great relationship all through the years, from the time that you started to walk to the time you started school, all the way through.

I think that our relationship has expanded a lot now, since you started Walter Panas [High School] and we started to study together. Do you remember the time we did American history?

**Mitchell:** Oh yes, I surely did. From what I can remember, I think it started from before when I was at Panas. Because sometimes before I started going to Panas that I used to go over to your house and we would go upstairs into the kitchen and you had helped me to study for my big exams or big tests that I may have and you always do that every time when I was in school.

Remember when we were studying together, whenever I misspell a word, you tell me to spell it correctly.... "Don't spell it wrong, spell it right!"

**Grandpa:** And I made you rewrite it. We did have some interesting times. We even had a few arguments, didn't we? During the study of American history and economics. Remember that?

Now discussions have evolved into other topics, such as politics, which I know you're interested in....

**Mitchell:** We talk about other things as well, like what I'm doing with myself, all the activities I've been doing, my job situation. We talk about many things....

**Grandpa:** Getting back to politics — even though our thinking has always been more conservative, yours and mine, but now that we have a new president-elect, what's your opinion about him? Do you think he'll be able to handle the job?

**Mitchell:** From my perspective, I think Bill Clinton is more than capable of handling the world affairs. To me ... he has the experience and the qualifications. In any case, I do feel that Clinton is the right person for the job.

**Grandpa:** Speaking about jobs, I think we both think that the major problem right now is to create more jobs....

**Mitchell:** Yes. That's one of the issues.... We need to exist by having trade with other countries. If we start having ... more free trade, then we can start creating new jobs for us.

**Grandpa:** We just had a wonderful Thanksgiving together. It was nice and friendly. After dinner and dessert, we sat around and chatted for over an hour. One of the strengths of the whole family is everyone's so compatible.

**Mitchell:** Speaking about compatibility, when I was thinking about your fiftieth wedding anniversary, to me that was a special moment because throughout my life with my relationship with you and Grandma that both of you always been there for me. Whenever I needed to talk about any problem I may had and many situations that may came up which I might not be comfortable discussing with my parents.

**Grandpa:** One of the interesting things about our family's relationship with one another is that there is no generation gap.

Even though I'm much older than you...we can talk almost on a friendly basis as if we were good friends — which we are. And I think that's very important....

**Mitchell:** There's another part of our relationship which we didn't touch on, which was sometimes when we get together, I'd make a list of some things we need and we may go out and do some shopping and getting stuff that I may need. Sometimes you need things yourself and you ask my opinion about those kinds of things.

**Grandpa:** That's true. We have talks about fashion, about style, about jeans, about sweaters, about shirts —

**Mitchell:** About refrigerators, about ties...

**Grandpa:** It's a lot of fun that way. You forgot to tell about how you introduced me to Burger King and the fish sandwich when we went to lunch.... That was the first time I was ever at Burger King. You were nice and ordered for me and brought the tray around for me. Those were good times.

**Mitchell:** Part of our relationship...this relationship is important to me because, to me, I look up to you on a lot of things.... I'm thinking about all the memories we went through throughout many years.... One of these special things was when doing my Bar Mitzvah when I was thirteen years old and Great Grandma gave me that kiddush cup. To me, that was important because...she reminded me how special my relationship was to my grandparents.

**Grandpa:** Tonight we were talking about your preference as to your future career, which I thought was also very interesting. Now you're working at the bank and you also have another job, but you find that the banking job is much more interesting for you, and you seem to enjoy it. Is that true?

**Mitchell:** Yes, that's true. Part of the reason why it is important is because of you.... You're the one who started in that field, in banking. Now you've been a director of People's Westchester Bank, which made it more interesting because of our relationship because now we could talk about the banking field.

**Grandpa:** That's true. We have a lot more in common to talk about, and now you're kind of following in my footsteps, right? A different generation is continuing in the same career.

**Mitchell:** My career is different than yours because I'm thinking about being in government. That is totally different than what your career was in banking. It's two different fields.

**Grandpa:** What part are you thinking about playing in government? I know you worked for Assemblyman George Pataki—

**Mitchell:** And Assemblywoman Maureen Ogden, too.

**Grandpa:** So you got a taste of what politics is like and the routine you have to follow and all the things you have to do. A lot of conversations with people and mailing. You have to let people know what's going on through the mail.

**Mitchell:** From what I remember, your side of the family, Grandpa, part of your family has been in government, too. Like Ed Gibbs and Fran.

**Grandpa:** I think what we were taught—for example, what my brother Ed and I were taught by our father—was that it's important to work at your career but it's also important to provide some sort of service to your community. And you can do it by either being involved in politics through an elected office or, in my case, I served on various boards, like the planning board, and the parking authority, and the urban renewal board. So you're participating in what's going on in your community and trying to make things better so that the next generation—which is you, Mitchell—will have a better place to live.

**Mitchell:** I'm thinking of doing the same thing.

**Grandpa:** Now you were talking about becoming an advocate for people with disabilities....

**Mitchell:** That's to help people's causes because there are many causes around today. What you said a few minutes ago about serving for your community, that's what I am really interested in doing. Because I've been doing that a lot by advocating for people with disabilities all the time.

**Grandpa:** You've gone to seminars and spoken about your particular feelings about having a disability and how you're coping with it and you're kind of advising people that they can cope with it, too. And you're also fighting in the legislature — you went to the Senate in Washington to speak about it —

**Mitchell:** To testify, which is more interesting.

**Grandpa:** I think your career is pretty well mapped out. It's just that you're going to take it one step at a time. You're starting at the bank and your other job, and it will expand as time goes on. You'll be doing more in your career, and also more in your service-type career, which will be as an advocate to help let the legislators know that certain things have to be done in education and job development for those people who have disabilities. Because they want to be self-sufficient, too. But they have to be given the opportunity....

**Mitchell:** That's one of the main issues. That we need many opportunities in order to succeed. Part of having many successes is part of what we do today that makes people proud of us.

**Grandpa:** And you may become proud of yourself because you may be achieving some things for other people besides yourself, some of whom you don't even know.

**Mitchell:** No matter if you're here or in Florida, we are always in communication. We always talk about many things and stating how important a relationship is to a person.

*December '92*

*The following is a conversation between Jason and his grandfather Alan Perl.*

**Jason:** The grandpa and grandson relationship. Well, he's like a teacher in some ways and he can teach me a lot of science, history, and recreational trips like I'm going to Spain. He's always teaching me some Spanish and some famous painters.

**Grandpa:** But don't you think a relationship is more than just teaching?

**Jason:** Yeah, in some ways. In our past he loved me a lot—and not just in the past.

I feel that Grandpa is a special person to be with.... You got my mom as a daughter. My mom has me. I'm your grandson.

**Grandpa:** You're nobody else's grandson but mine. That's special.

**Jason:** Special and loving....

**Grandpa:** It would be good if all grandfathers felt the same way about their grandsons that I feel about you. My interest in you is a very special interest. I don't have anybody else that I have the kind of relationship that I have with you. It's a combination of love, trying to make you the kind of person I think you'll be happiest as, to give you some idea of what I think are the important values for your whole life.

**Jason:** And it's not only love is our relationship.

**Grandpa:** That's part of it. The things we do together are part of my attempt to make you happier and better, better able to be a good person in the world.

You see, I didn't have a grandpa. My two grandpas died when I was very young. I'm lucky I have a grandson I can communicate with, have fun with, talk to, and watch grow up.

Let's review some of the things we've done together.

**Jason:** Like when we fished together.

**Grandpa:** You had never gone fishing before, had you?

**Jason:** No.

**Grandpa:** Why did we do that?

**Jason:** You wanted to make me happier.

**Grandpa:** I wanted to show you something you could do for the rest of your life. Did it work out?

**Jason:** Yeah, it was fun. I remember that we went to Montauk.... We went to see the sand dunes and we made a land-mark and you taught me how to tie my shoes the right way. And learning to eat new foods.

**Grandpa:** Do you remember the walks we used to take?... Remember how we started to collect leaves from different kinds of trees and —

**Jason:** We made a book of the leaves: oak, red oak, maple, white maple....

**Grandpa:** Remember how I tried to show you how to make different kinds of knots?

**Jason:** Square knots, overhand, slip knots. And then later we had science experiments like magnets, like the north pole and south pole.

Our first experiment was how to make a compass.... When ships want to know where to go, they use a magnet with a small bowl of water and a —

**Grandpa:** A needle. We had two magnets —

**Jason:** And you told me like poles would repel and opposite poles would attract.

**Grandpa:** Then we made a compass. We took a needle and put the needle on the magnet and made it float on water, and the needle pointed to —

**Jason:** North!

**Grandpa:** Remember our first experiment about weighing the air?

**Jason:** Sure.

**Grandpa:** How did we find out that air has weight?

**Jason:** Those two balloons. One with air and one without air. The one with air weighed more, and the one without air weighed less.

**Grandpa:** And we had to test that with a balance scale, which we made ourselves.

**Jason:** We also had our box called Physics. Oh yeah, and my measuring experiments.

**Grandpa:** First we took a tape and measured a table, and then a room.

**Jason:** We measured the room, the kitchen. And then we measured the whole house.

**Grandpa:** Do you remember how we could measure the height of the ceiling without going up to the ceiling? We used a triangle for that, and what else?

**Jason:** A protractor.

**Grandpa:** Right. My, you learned a lot.

**Emily:** Grandpa's done a lot of reading to you.

**Jason:** "Just So Stories" and something about a long fish called a latimeria. Latimeria was the oldest fish in the world.

**Grandpa:** Remember we talked about the prehistoric men? And I gave you part of my collection of fossils.

**Jason:** Arrowheads and rocks. And rock and shell collections.

**Grandpa:** We also had a lot of fun playing word games. We used to play knock-knock jokes.

**Jason:** Like spelling games, puns, homographs, homophones — yeah.

**Grandpa:** I used to do the same games with your mom and your uncle Danny when they were young.

There are some things I did with you that I couldn't have done without you. I wouldn't have gone to Wig 'n' Whiskers. I enjoyed seeing you perform. I went to your graduation. I was very proud to see you graduate.

**Jason:** From middle school?

**Emily:** And next year —

**Jason:** I graduate from high school!

**Grandpa:** And I'll be there! Another thing we've done is, I used to conduct the Seder for the family — not just the family. The Capones, the Hutchings, and other friends were there, too.

**Jason:** I remember the way you hid the matzo and didn't want me to look at it.

**Grandpa:** And sometimes you found it and sometimes other people found it.

**Jason:** I found it two times. One was over the piano in the music box, and one time it was hid in a hat.... You tried to make me eat new things—like the horseradish—and the bitter stuff that made my ears smoke....

**Grandpa:** Remember the museums we went to?

**Jason:** Like the Magritte exhibit.

**Grandpa:** Yes, and the dinosaurs.

**Jason:** At the Museum of Natural History. And the big blue whale up on the ceiling.

**Grandpa:** You're getting ready to go to Spain now. We had a talk about some of the artists you're going to see there.

**Jason:** Goya, and Velázquez, and—

**Grandpa:** El Greco and Murillo—

**Jason:** And Bosch.

**Grandpa:** You know what the Spaniards call Bosch? You know his first name? It's a funny name. Geronimus. In English that's Jerome. Jerry Bosch. The Spanish call him El Bosco.

**Jason:** ...A long time ago, I think Grandma Florence was a great artist. I remember Grandma Florence. Some of the memories about her: She was loving you. I was on her lap.

**Grandpa:** She loved you plenty.

**Jason:** She had knit a sweater for my mom and a hat. And she saw me swim a lot.

**Grandpa:** She watched everything you did.

I think maybe I started you on a lot of things. How far you go is up to you. Oh—we forgot the stamps.

**Jason:** The stamp collecting. The U.S.A. and Europe and some of the foreign stuff. The location of the different countries. How much money are they.

**Emily:** And how about the astronomy?

**Jason:** Looking at stars: at Orion, North Star, and Big Dipper and Polaris.

**Grandpa:** We talked a lot about how far away the stars are.

**Jason:** We went to the planetarium.

**Grandpa:** Let me ask you something. How did you like the concert of "The Messiah" the other night? . . .

**Jason:** It was fun. It was long. I enjoyed the music. Some of the high music makes me happy. Some of the low music makes me teary eyed. It's like magical emotion. Some feelings change in some ways. . . . Happy music and soothing relaxed music and then it comes up to a bright waltz. And some of it I had tears in my eyes. Like I felt like bursting into tears at some parts. Like water, big puddles of water over the whole building.

**Grandpa:** We have to listen to more music like that together, really good music, and see what it means to you. We haven't done too much of that. I've been very proud of *your* attempts at music.

**Jason:** It's spiritual-like. Some of the music I like makes me feel like dancing. . . . In my life I did piano about four years and violin for two years. And Dad brought me a harmonica and a recorder. I love music.

**Grandpa:** One thing we have to do—you should play your instrument and I'll play the recorder with you. We can play together.

**Jason:** I would like to do that.

**Grandpa:** We could do a trio. You and Mom and me.

**Jason:** I had a concert. You came to the concert at Mort Ross's when I played the violin. Mom had the camcorder.

**Grandpa:** I'd like to do some more serious reading with you. I think you're ready to understand some more serious stuff now.

**Jason:** I'd like to do some science fiction stories. Like "Earth to the Moon." Or *Twenty Thousand Leagues under the Sea*.

**Grandpa:** I'd like to get you involved in the Greek myths. You know what myths are? They're something like fairy tales. But these were the stories the Greeks read and told to their children about the Greek heroes and Greek gods. There was a famous Greek hero named Jason.

**Jason:** Me?

**Grandpa:** Not you — but a Greek hero with the same name as you.

**Jason:** I was trying to look in the dictionary to find the meaning of my name. Looks like I was in the Argonaut.

**Grandpa:** "Jason and the Golden Fleece." That's a great story. The other things I'd like to try with you is to go . . . to Philadelphia together. The Declaration of Independence was signed there —

**Jason:** And the Articles of Confederation.

**Grandpa:** We're going to go to where the Declaration of Independence was actually signed and the Liberty Bell —

**Jason:** Is cracked . . . in 1776.

**Grandpa:** Well I think we've had some pretty good times together. I think we'll have a lot more now that you're growing up. You're a voter now. By the way, did you vote for the right candidate? Did your man win?

**Jason:** Yep . . . my man wins.

**Grandpa:** You think he'll make a good president?

**Jason:** Yes, I think he will. Because he has a good record.

**Grandpa:** He's interested in handicapped people. He's interested in the common people.

**Jason:** People like me and Mitchell. Probably after the book comes out, I was thinking Clinton might read the book.

**Grandpa:** I think if you send him a copy of it, it would be nice.

**Jason:** Clinton might tell the news to announce to all of our country and all the world to read our book.

**Grandpa:** That would certainly help sales. . . .

**Jason:** . . . I feel like Grandpa is very fond of me. . . . He's been a great grandpa ever since I was young. Since this time right now, I feel that he's the best guy I ever had.

If I didn't have this Down syndrome business . . . there are some things that I like to teach Grandpa about. . . .

**Grandpa:** I know a lot more about Down syndrome than I

ever did before. I think you've made a tremendous contribution to Down syndrome and handicapped people all over the world by being who you are.

**Jason:** The things we've been doing has always been making me more smart.... I learned a lot from you and a lot from my experience.

**Grandpa:** I only helped a little bit. I think we can continue our relationship on a much more grown-up level now. There are so many things to enjoy, and we can enjoy them together, and I can help you to understand them....

**Jason:** Not only are there the things we've [been] doing together, I can now do more things independently.

**Emily:** There are some things that you might not want to do with a mom or dad but you *would* do them with a grandpa.

**Grandpa:** For example, if you had a problem you wanted to discuss with someone, and you didn't want to talk to Mom or Dad, I'd be a good person to talk to.

**Jason:** I think this whole thing about a relationship with a grandpa-grandson relationship is to keep right on going even though I have problems.

**Grandpa:** Next time you have a real tough problem, try me out. Here's an example. Suppose you had a problem and you didn't know how to handle it and you felt bad. That's a good thing you could come to me about.... We could talk about it and maybe find a different way of handling it.

**Jason:** Hard problems that I may be stuck at... I can talk to you. Some things are easy I can work out myself. The ones I don't know the answer to, I need help.

**Grandpa:** Try me out. You'll find because we have such a good relationship, we can talk about anything — anything under the sun. No matter how personal, no matter how complicated — you know I'll keep it to myself and we'll work it out together.

**Jason:** Actually some of those simple problems I can work out... but if I can't, then I need you.

**Grandpa:** Depends on what the problem is. There are certain kinds of problems that are so intimate and personal, you're embarrassed to talk about. That's what grandpas are best at.

**Jason:** Grandpas are smart.

**Grandpa:** Not only that. I've had a lot of experience.... If you've lived as long as I have, you'll find there's some very good advice you can get. You can even get advice on how to get independent. If you want to keep it confidential, I'm your guy. I can do a lot for you, and I can keep my mouth shut.

**Jason:** It's like you're on the same team that I'm on.

**Grandpa:** You're right. Exactly. I'm the number one guy on your team. You want to run with the ball, but you may need somebody to block for you.

**Emily:** Sounds like you guys love each other a lot.

**Grandpa:** I think we do.

**Jason:** I think we do, too.

**Grandpa:** I'm going through a difficult stage now. I need some help, too.

**Jason:** I can help you, and you can help me.

**Emily:** Grandpa hasn't lived alone in a long time. He's lonely now, since Susan passed away.

**Jason:** I can help with that.... It's a hard subject of dying.

**Grandpa:** That's something to talk about, too.

**Jason:** I'm not thinking of dying when I'm this age.

**Grandpa:** You shouldn't. Strangely, I don't think about dying at *this* age.

**Jason:** Maybe when you're in the high nineties ...

**Grandpa:** You know it's coming, but you don't think about it.

**Emily:** That's good.

**Grandpa:** I love you, Jason.

**Jason:** I love you, too.

**Grandpa:** You're a nice person. I don't mean you're a perfect person. But you're the kind of person I like to know. The kind of person I'd like to be.

# 10
# Beliefs, Traditions, Loss, and Grief

## "Calmly Relaxing Angel"

*February '91*

**Emily:** Jason, what do you know about religion?

**Jason:** Well, religion means your beliefs and customs, passed down in your ancestors. That's what the meaning is.

What it means to me that there is a God up in heaven makes everything in this whole universe. And I believe that. I thought the nebular theory makes the universe, but who makes the nebular theory?

My grandpa is Jewish, and Mom and Dad and my aunts and uncles and our whole family.... You are Jewish. How come you are not sure if there is a God or not?

**Emily:** I am Jewish because all of my ancestors were Jewish, and I love the history and the tradition of being Jewish. I love the holidays and the foods and music. But I'm just not sure about the God part. Can you understand that?

**Jason:** I could understand that if I know what you're saying.

**Emily:** How come you feel so sure that there *is* a God?

**Jason:** Well, look around you! Who made that printer? Who made the chairs? Who made the house? Who made the country? Who made the government and the president?

**Emily:** ... I'm not sure who made all those things. Mostly I think *people* made them. Especially the chairs. I have more trouble when you ask me who made flowers.

**Jason:** Yeah, who made 'em? What makes history and prehistoric history? Who made the big bang theory and the nebular theory? I don't believe shock waves make the nebular theory.

**Emily:** So you figure there must be a God to have started it all off, right?

**Jason:** Yes.

### July '91

*Jason's grandmother "Nana K." (Charles's mother) died on July 17, 1991, the day before her ninety-seventh birthday. She had been in a nursing home for about a year. Jason visited with her every two or three weeks. He fed her, talked to her, even brought his violin to play for her.*

*Jason came home from summer camp for his grandmother's funeral. The next day, he returned to camp and wrote the following birthday card to her:*

> I dreamt last night that you are in heaven,
>     calmly relaxing angel.
> In our hands we'll be loving you forever.
> You mean so much to us.
> When you are dead or alive we need you in peace.
>                                   *Your heavenly Jason K.*

### September '92

**Jason:** We have our illness of the family. My grandpa's [Alan Perl's] girlfriend which is a friend of mine, named Sue Gilman, and she is very sick, very weak, and she thinks she is going to die. She has cancer.

When I came home from camp, I came to see her in the Phelps Hospital. When I came in, she says, "What a lovely surprise," and she said something that didn't make any sense like

"Happy Birthday, Happy Wedding. Happy Happy Happy." I think she was happy to see me. Maybe she thinks that I have a beautiful future when she says "Happy Wedding." I gave her a hug and a kiss.

Now it is three weeks later and she is struggling and never feel pain. When the family came to see Sue . . . I thought that was fun while the family was there, fun to see our family, but it was not a fun occasion. And this is how the trouble started.

Just as the family said good-bye to Sue, without me in the room, I was in the hall. I'm going to try to see her for one last moment to say good-bye to Sue. Grandpa suggested that I should be thinking about her when she was alive. Mom told me that it was my decision, but Grandpa didn't want me to get in the room. He was overprotective. He was to protect my feelings. He thinks it would be a bad memory for me to think about Sue. He wants me to think of good stuff, what happened in the last few years that she was healthy and alive and not think of how she looked now in the hospital. So I didn't go in.

But I feel real angry about what Grandpa was saying because I wanted to see Sue and I wanted to say a last moment of saying good-bye to her. Grandpa still says that I have to think about good stuff about her. So I was upset.

So I talked to Vito, my psychologist, about how to face a fear of death, and I hope you'll listen, too. It's not easy to face the fear of death, but you have to think about the good stuff about the people and share our memories. Vito helped me to understand the way people die in a certain age and start to think that it's not a good environment for you to be in. We have to learn of facing fear and moving on from there.

After Vito, I decided to go there to see her and say good-bye. When we got there to the hospital, we saw Grandpa. Grandpa told us she was in a bad way. She was struggling with her breathing. He didn't want to see it, and he said that we shouldn't see it either because it was so horrible, so sad.

So he convinced me not to go in the room. So we went for a walk instead. And I helped Grandpa share a lot of memories of a lot of people I handled over a lot of my life.

Some of the memories are: Nana K. — when we visited at the nursing home before she died, we always bring her pastrami sandwiches because she had no teeth. She loved it and also I brought my violin to play for her in the nursing home, and she loved that, too.

I told Grandpa about Sue Gilman — the memories are she gave me a Read-Along tape of *Wizard of Oz*, fishing together, we went to Montauk with Alejandra, climbing up sandy mountains, and she is always very nice to me and she loved me.

I told him that Grandma Florence sat with me at picnics, a nice sweater that she knitted for Mom, and I put my head on her shoulder. I stood on the rock [outside the hospital] and waved to her window.

Then Grandpa told me sometimes he gets into that age that his time will come, too. So I told him I have lots of memories of him — trying to eat new things, fishing together at Gedney Park, my science experiments, my rock collections, my leaf collection, helped me with my American history, and lots more. I love him.

I hugged him, I put my arms around him and he cried, and I was a smart person because I helped him. And he said to me that was a smart decision to make, not to go to the room for Sue. And I said I would remember her when she was alive.

I once believed that I can make things happen quickly and easy. That's my only wish. I told Grandpa my wish would be when we leave the hallway, one voice out of the distance would come out saying a nice perfect accent and when we turned around it was Sue all along, that she was back.

He said that would be very nice, but if all the dead people came back it would be very crowded. I'm not saying that to him. I'm saying all the people that we know *in our family* could be back alive and the other people who have died can be on their own. Just wondered if Jack Lipton, Grandma Florence, Aunt Edith, Uncle Jesse could come back alive so everyone could come back and live at the same time and never think about dying and that's it.

It's nice to see movies about dying because it's fun for me and it's relaxing instead of real life because in the movies people who die come back as ghosts, spirits, and souls. From *Beetlejuice*, Adam and Barbara came back. In *Ghost*, Karl, Willie Lopez, and Sam came back. In *Defending Your Life*, Albert Brooks came back and moved on....

In real life people doesn't come back. It would be nice if they did. That would be a good boundary. But they don't. So we miss them. We remember them. And that's how they come back.

*August '92*

*The following section was written by Mitchell.*

I feel that my views about my religion and heritage are an important part of my life. When I go to services and read the prayers, I believe what they tell me. The Bible is a part of this as well. God is important to me in many ways....

The values of religion, faith, and heritage were taught to me by my family and other important people who I cared about. Part of religion that is fun is that we celebrate the holidays with my family and friends.... I believe in the meaning and the importance of the holidays. That means a commitment to me and I enjoy those times.

These views about religion were of major importance to me when I was Bar Mitzvahed. I believed it was a part of my life to be religious and to believe what I felt when I was Bar Mitzvahed.... I was capable to read and chant this Hebrew language.... I was taught by my Hebrew school teachers and the rabbi that after being a Bar Mitzvah is to be an adult and to continue believing what religion means to you. [It] was a very special part of my life to fill the dream that my father had that he saw his son became an adult.

*November '92*

**Mitchell:** At my Bar Mitzvah, my great grandmother gave me a kiddush cup, and that was very special to me. Because I realized how important she was and how special she was to me because she was always there to talk to or to listen to about anything. The relationship I have with her is very special because I realize how important my ancestors were to me even though I wasn't born at the time.

...Part of being part of a family is our heritage. Where we get our values from. Our values come from our ancestors: grandparents to parents to you. It's an important concept.

Part of a relationship or friendship is built on the importance of family because families can help each other out in many situations. By going in the past, by realizing...how important our ancestors were to our parents' life. If it was that important to them, they will share their experience with us to learn more about the family, to learn about those experiences.

**Jason:** There's something about ancestors that you didn't even think about in the future. How about your grandparents go to your parents and your parents go to you and you can pass it down to your children in the future?

**Mitchell:** Part of this is in every generation. There will be a new child comes along, there's a tradition that every family has.

Let me give you one example. At every Bar or Bat Mitzvah in our family we do this toast that one generation to another share a special glass of brandy and drink a toast to life. This tradition had been started by my father's mom and dad at *his* Bar Mitzvah.

Because to me life and the generations and tradition is the way we feel not only about our ancestors but the way we feel about our perspective, our feelings about what happened in the past.

To me, I was not around when my father's father died. I was not...born then. But [my father] did ask me once to go to the cemetery with him where his father was buried so that I know how important his relationship was to his father.

...To me it is important to learn about the experience he had as a son to a father.... It gave me an impression that I want to build a good relationship with my father because my father is important to me, just as he was to his father.

**Jason:** Traditions and beliefs can pass down to the future because it starts with parents. The values of parents get passed to me and that's what's happening now. Now I have lots of great importances. But now I have that same values as my parents, I can teach it to my future kids when I get married.

**Mitchell:** Tradition is very important to me because I feel I want to follow in my family tradition steps because it makes me feel that tradition is part of my life. Life is important because I feel that the traditions that my family went through was important to them and I want to continue on that same path.

# 11
# Politics and World Affairs
## "Citizens of All the World"

*February '91*

**Emily:** You have been following the news of the [Gulf] War closely.

**Mitchell:** Yes, that's correct.

**Emily:** And how do you feel about what we are doing over there?

**Mitchell:** I would say at this point of time we have the greatest advantage in air supremacy. So far we knocked out half of the Iraqi military and their equipment. We had also hit 30 percent of their tanks. I believe that we should not . . . negotiate with the Iraqis because the more time we negotiate, the more time the Iraqis will have to restore themselves. So I believe the peace initiative that the Soviets made out should fail. The ground war should be in effect at any moment.

**Jason:** I think this is a very tense war. We should go into the war. Because we're so much worrying about our friends and family in Israel and there are some cities have less food because they have less money so it is affected on us so we should . . . go and have this war so we won't have that kind of problem again.

**Mitchell:** Do you think, do you agree with what the United

States is doing at this time? In your answer can you not just say anything about the linkage with the Israeli problem?

**Jason:** I know what Iraq did. Iraq went and put oil in the ocean, and that's a mean thing to do. We should get some factories to clean oil out and not have that problem. I think Iraq invading Kuwait is not very good at all. I still think that Iraqis should move out.

**Mitchell:** Do you think the Iraqis should withdraw from Kuwait unconditionally?

**Jason:** They should go back where they came from and Iraqis will get a blockade, which means Iraqis won't move back into Kuwait. So we separate them and that's it.

**Mitchell:** I'm going to add a couple of things to that. The problem is the invasion of Kuwait — it's not about Israel's policy and problem. It all has to do with just Kuwait. What the Iraqis are doing, they're trying to push the Israeli problem into this war by having this linkage. But if they seriously think to negotiate by getting out of this war, they should do it unconditionally so that the Iraqis should overthrow the Iraqi government. What Saddam Hussein is doing, he wants to be leader of all of the Arabs. But I don't think it's going to work. The only way we can stop Saddam Hussein is to get total control of air supremacy. If that doesn't work, we should use a ground war attack on the Iraqis. But eventually the Iraqis have the advantage because the missiles that they have. This will affect many casualties.

**Emily:** Reading and hearing about the war in Iraq, do you ever think about the war coming here to the United States?

**Mitchell:** It is possible, but realistically their SCUD missiles cannot come over here because we're looking at two separate countries on two different sides of the world. Their missiles cannot reach the U.S. at all. We have to look at this war so that we could end all dictatorships.

**Jason:** Yes, this reminds me that if the SCUD missiles *could* reach the United States, it can affect different parts of New York and the United States. It would be like all these soldiers of Iraq could take over the United States. That would be horrible. I was thinking before this war comes to the United States, we should plan ahead. Instead of them coming here and [gas] getting in the house without planning, we should get tape on our doors and lock all windows and the chimney so it won't get in.

**Mitchell:** Jason, there are things you have to remember. What you're saying about — if this war did end up here in the United States, there will be many damages. More importantly, this will affect the economy. The economy is where all the money is stored to help the citizens and to budget our monies for safety. Because right now we are in a recession. With this in mind, and the cost of the Operation Desert Storm, it will mean more problems, more cutbacks. We still have the faith in the future.

**Emily:** We got a letter from our friends in Israel which described the way they are living through this war. They have one room which they have sealed off in case of a chemical gas attack. All the people have been issued gas masks. In the middle of the night, the sirens go off and it is an air raid. The people have to get out of bed, put on their gas masks, and go into their sealed room. The room has tape around the windows and doors so no gas can come in.

**Mitchell:** What you're saying is that this will protect the people from getting hurt or injured or gassed. It probably is very — living like hell.... They may be confused. They don't know what's going on. The journalists who are there in Israel they are telling us what's going on so that we know what the information and background so we know that our friends and our families are safe. But we still have to remember that there are going to be damages that have to be rebuilt.

**Jason:** I think it's very scary and dark. You can't live — you can die from chemicals and nuclear gas.

**Mitchell:** They could very easily die if they throw poison gas.

It could also cause problems for the country...because it may take some time, they may have to stay in the shelters until it's over.

It's very tragic, it's sad, it's very emotional to a lot of people. Because all the people who are at fault in wars before went through a very emotional time. We should reflect on those times and reflect on those men and women who fought those wars before.... Those lives have touched our hearts and our memories.

Jason, in the future, are you planning on being in the armed forces?

**Jason:** Well that's a good point you got there. My uncle Al was in the air force once in 1942, when the World War Two has been going on. And he gave me a jacket with an air force insignia on it. Sometime I [can] go to an army college.... Someday, yeah.

**Mitchell:** Can you tell us when that someday will be?

**Jason:** It depends on how the war is going on. If they withdraw soon, I don't go to the armed forces because the war will be ended soon. If the war will be late, I should go in the middle of it and probably I can make them to go out or withdraw from Kuwait or get some SCUD missiles in Iraq so the Iraqis move out of Kuwait.

**Mitchell:** I have to say that I have mixed feelings going into the army...because I feel my family comes first and that I do want to lead my nation, but I feel what's more important is to be with my family. Because I see very rarely a person with a disability goes into the army—because they have lack of experience to hit the prime targets that the United States wants to hit. So I think it's a bit premature to go into the army...because of lack of experience, and I feel that I want to have a future of my own and to understand about the world. The world is important to me, but the situation in the Persian Gulf is a very complicated issue and that's why I do not want to be in the army for these reasons.

*October '92*

**Jason:** Last night I was watching the debates between Clinton, Bush, and Perot. They wanted to make America into a better place. They all want to become president. And so far Clinton's ideas made me happy to vote for him.

The problem with Bush is that he was about foreign policy. Problems with Perot that he thinks about economics, he didn't make any sense. He always has a good sense of humor. I think Clinton is making issues more serious and not that funny.

And I was thinking to make this America to be a better place.

If I were president I would change America into a brighter, clean, and fun future for all citizens.

First things first, that we should start off with clean bridges. Some people are writing graffiti on the bridges.

[We need] to make better schools for children, and for teenagers, too, and even people doing drugs and cigarettes can even learn how not to drink and not to smoke because that's the beginning of destroying their life. They need more education.

They need also to learn how to keep an employment job and to be smart. The more you learn in school, the better citizens you can be and the better jobs they can get. When people don't get education, they will be poor because they are not experiencing the real world of jobs. If they don't have jobs, they'll be poor and increase poverty.

Another thing... drivers can learn how to be good citizens so they can drive better. I went out to see the road and see if there's any stupid drivers there. And I saw plenty of them. And I think what I should do to make this America better is that all those crazy drivers will learn not to be crazy drivers. They all have to go to driver education school.

For a good start of good drivers, we'll have more of those yield signs and stop signs and good signals. And more supervision of cops because if one person is disobeying a law, they might get a ticket until they get into arrest. Cops would be more strict for bad drivers or drivers who disobey laws.

If I would be one of the debaters, I would be president. Wow. I think people would like my ideas. I'd be the top of Clinton, Bush, and Perot together. America would be a nice, clean, ozone-locked, in a peace-making world.

In Israel what they should do is to get along to each other. The Arabs and the Jews have to agree they have to live together in peace.... If they agree, they'll too be citizens of all the world.

But not only Israelis and Arabs. All the people all over the world can be citizens of the world. Not only Europe. South America, North America, Asia, Europe, Africa, Australia, and, oh yeah, Antarctica.

We are worried about the people who are starving in Africa. We are worried about war in Russia. We are worried about the poverty in South America. We are worried about problems in the students in China. Any other countries in other continents can be citizens of the whole planet.

One other topic I forgot to mention is AIDS and diseases that harms the people. And pollution, too.

We need some more education on AIDS programs so people can learn how to prevent AIDS and protect their own bodies. Then we need more doctors to be working on more strong strong medicines.

Don't say this cannot be true: my invention. My invention is "AIDS Reliever." This invention is a medicine and it cures AIDS. I wish I can invent this. They will go to the hospital after the day, take their blood, and now it's normal. And that would be great.

My invention will have to be mixed with a lot of liquids like Tylenol, Sudafed, DayQuil and NyQuil, and some other liquids you drink a lot—like water, ginger ale, apple juice, grape juice, Sunkist. It can help to fight the disease in the blood to make more clean blood. The reason why is because after the drink's digested in the stomach, it goes into the bloodstream to fight the blood.

I will not recommend to say if my invention doesn't work, then nothing I can do about it. But I wish it would.

One of my puppeteers in "Sesame Street," Richard Hunt, died from AIDS. He was a good pal. He played Forgetful Jones in that show, and I appeared with him a lot. I really loved him. And I miss him. I went to his funeral and told him that we share a lot of good memories.

There's another person — on "Life Goes On," one of the characters is Jesse who has AIDS, and I was thinking what Jesse would have to learn was to have to live in a nice clean world what I said before. It bothers me that Jesse might get sick and die. I wish Jesse can also take my invention and get better.

Another thing to make the world a better place is to have less pollution. One thing that makes less pollution is less cars, less machines, and less factories making smoke.

And more recycling. We want to recycle bottles, newspapers, handy papers, plastic, rubber, plastic bottles, aluminum cans, aluminum bottles, etc. One rule, and this can be silly, is anyplace you litter, there must be one garbage can there for you. Parents will tell their children not to throw until we find a garbage can.... If you want to throw a paper out of the car, you have to stop the car and put it in the garbage can or find a garbage can, aim at it, and toss it in.

We will have a cleaner and wise and much more safer and beautiful world.

And disabled and Down syndrome people can also be good citizens of the world. They may have problems, but they may have contributions to contribute for the rest of the world to be proud of.

America can be made better so the next generation of the upcoming children will have a nice community and experience the real nice world to live in. Not only peace but more safety, happiness, and to make a good environment.

Boy, if Clinton read this chapter he would say, "This person, Jason Kingsley, eighteen years old with Down syndrome, made a contribution to this world.... I thought Al Gore was helping me. Now I got another partner, Jason Kingsley." That would be a great miracle.

**Jason:** Hello, this is Jason Kingsley for CBS News ... for Down Syndrome News. Mitchell, what is your ideas about the presidential election?

**Mitchell:** Most people want to stick to the issues at large. The issues at large are done with many factors. One is family values. Two about health. Three, economy. Four, jobs.

These areas are very important to every American today in the world. Many of us has a plan, and all the plans are laid out in Washington, D.C. But in any case, not every plan always works out because between the Congress and the president there are no cooperation.

We are now in gridlock, and we want to end this gridlock by having a new Congress. Having a new Congress, we could get much more done to help the people — to create new jobs, to have a much better health system, and to help people in the economy.

Now, let's go into specifics, regarding the debates. I believe that Bill Clinton is not telling the truth. If he raised taxes in Arkansas, he may raise taxes to American taxpayers.

To me it's a flip-flop. Clinton will say one thing, then he'll say another. He'll make promises, but he will not follow the promises. If we make promises and do not keep the promises, what will the American people say? I'm not an expert, but I can say that we need a president who will help the people. It's time for a change and time for a renewal. That's why I believe George Bush is a better president.

Number one: Who can we trust in a crisis? In any situation or in any case. Two: Character. President Bush has better character than Bill Clinton. Want to know why? I'll tell you why. Bill Clinton in Arkansas has the lowest-rated jobs in America. In his state. He said $160 million will be cut in the middle class....

I think it is time to stop the cutting of the taxes. What we need is a country that will stick to the issues at large.

Besides the taxes here, how about the issue of jobs? Today people are losing jobs. In every position. To me, we need to create new jobs because of the unemployment is going up. The only way to create jobs is to have free trade with other countries. If we have free trade with other countries, we will get what we need and they'll get what they need by exporting.

...I have reason to believe that Bush is a better candidate to be reelected because...he was talking about family values. This is one major point in this campaign, because family is a very strong target. Family with children needs help. They need for their children for the best education. I think that parents and children would choose where they want to go to school. It's about choice. To me choice is a very important issue. If we do not have a choice to choose what we want, government will be in control. I think we should limit the government from making decisions.

For example, the decision of abortion. That should not be an issues. Not on the Supreme Court. I believe in ... Roe v. Wade and women's rights. I think a woman should decide whether to have a child or not. Because it is not an issue of the Supreme Court or any of our government leaders to decide. But what we can do to help them is to give them the information that they need, regarding to help them to make a decision. Not to make the decision for them. That they should make the decision for themselves.

Besides the issues of abortion, there is another one which is very serious.... Many people are dying because they haven't had any plan in Washington benefiting people with AIDS.... I hope we can find a cure for the virus and save more people from dying because of AIDS. I admire Magic Johnson speaking out and saying that he has the HIV virus. It takes a lot of courage for a person to speak out about something like this. It shows how important these people are to us. It proves to us that the government should do something for those individuals who need the help.

The other important issue in the political specter today is dealing with race. People are being discriminated because of their background. To me I feel it is time to have laws written down because of the diversity of races in the world.

I agree with health. I agree with Clinton and Bush because I believe in health care that we need. What we need is a better health care system....

Ross Perot to me may be a good candidate for president, but he does not know how to fix. He says he's going to go to Washington, D.C., and fix everything all out. To me, it's not about fixing it. It's about changing the way people see the views.

The debates went very well. I believe that because they stick to the issues, they stick to what is important to what they want to discuss. It establish what they want to be covered. Help people make up their minds who they want to support.

For me, I believe... there is no problem with President Bush with foreign policy. No matter what happens. For example, the Gulf War, Panama, the hostages in Libya. All those things happened in Bush's administration. To me, I think what Bush did for people is correct.

**Jason:** Perot, Bush, and Clinton did not raise an issue on people with disabilities. It might be a good topic for them to say about the ADA [Americans with Disabilities Act]. Discrimination against workers with disabilities. They are focused on making America into a better country. But they didn't mention what disabled would do to change America.

**Mitchell:** ...I heard President Bush about the ADA. Not in depth, not in detail. But he did. But the ADA is a start. There are other ways of dealing with issues with people with disabilities. You said you heard no one mention the ADA. I did.

They want to stick to the issues. For example: economy, jobs, health care, the environment. Those are the issues they want to talk on. They are the issues important to America.

I've heard when they do the commentary, they ask the people, the voters, what are they more impressive of and what they heard and what impressed them and what made them change their vote. They indicated what needs to be touched on. It's the voter who counts.

I think we need someone in government who is experienced in this field and has the knowledge. To me, I may be one of the people who can because not only that I have a disability, but I am feeling very strongly about people with disabilities and what they have to offer.

**Emily:** I understand that Clinton has a good record on disability issues, but even more important than that, I heard that he has several key people on his staff who have disabilities. That seems to me to be putting his money where his mouth is.

**Mitchell:** But Clinton—you just said there are people on his staff who have disabilities, but if this is the case, why didn't he say anything about it? I don't know. Bush signed a piece of legislation into law.

Education. People with disabilities attend schools and the education is an issue that is being discussed. Because we want better education for our children because they are going to be our next generation to come. I don't want to get off the subject, but eventually education is a strong issue because part of education is helping them, sharpening their skills, why it's important to have an education.

**Jason:** My opinion about education is they have to get more new classes of issues about the world and forget the academics part. Right now in this world people are dying and they don't care. Education is to have more classes about politics, about drunken driving, about AIDS, about how to say no to drugs, marijuana and crack and smoking. We want more of *those* classes of those issues of the world. Take away some of those math and history and concentrate on this.

**Mitchell:** Now in education, we need math and we need history. That's part of the young people learning about America. We don't need to have more classes because we have enough classes. We need to expand the curriculum. The curriculum needs to be expanded instead of having more classes.

**Barbara:** What do you think about the vice-presidential candidates?

**Jason:** I like Gore better. He's a partner of Clinton and he's more focused on many issues that help Clinton to learn about the world....

He is about the environment. If Clinton and Gore sit down together to tell him about the environment. Because we need both parts. One is how people would change the environment. That's one mixture of Gore and Clinton. Or Clinton might say, "What kind of community or kind of environment would we put people into a specially good government?"

**Mitchell:** To me, that I do not like Gore because of his stand on the environment.... But I do like Quayle because he's absolutely correct on many things. He's not misleading like Gore. He sticks to the issues. That's why I believe Bush and Quayle will have four more years.

**Jason:** I think Clinton and Gore — because we need two parts of the world to become a better place. Gore will tell what would happen about saving the planet.... And Clinton says what would be the actions of the people who will be in the government.

**Mitchell:** ... I think Bush and Quayle are going to win because of the issues. They have more understanding of the issues and more experience than Bill Clinton and Al Gore.

I have reason to believe that Bush and Quayle are telling

the truth and Bill Clinton and Al Gore doesn't tell the truth. Who can we trust in a crisis? Who has experience in the field? Bush and Quayle. Because they know the issues at large and what needs to be focused on. I believe with the ticket of Bush and Quayle is a better ticket because they know what we need is better economy, more jobs, free trade, better health care system. Those are the important issues that will be addressed when he is reelected as president. Let me continue.

**Jason:** What you're saying about more jobs, do you mean you'll have more jobs in a clean world? Or less jobs to close down some of that smoke?

**Mitchell:** I'm not talking about jobs in the environment. I'm talking about jobs in general. Not in combination with the environment.

**Barbara:** But what about the environment?

**Mitchell:** It will be an issue, and it will be addressed. First they discuss the important issues first. Environment is important issue, but the other issues are more important issues to be discussed first.

**Emily:** If these guys are so up on the important issues and have so much experience, how come the first four years didn't do much and the country is in pretty bad shape?

**Mitchell:** Because we've had a lot of plans surrounding Washington. It's not Bush's fault. It's Congress's fault. The Democratic liberals. Because they're not cooperating with the president. If the Congress cannot do it, then Bush should have a chance of doing it himself. Then getting an approval from the Congress to approve it. We do not need pork-barrel legislation.

The issue of trust and character. Right now, we do not trust Clinton and Gore because they made promises and they break their promises.

He's promising people a tax cut. He's making all sorts of promises, and he won't keep them. I think Bush and Quayle are going to win no matter what.

**Jason:** I think Clinton and Gore will win because *some* people can trust Clinton and Gore.

**Mitchell:** Jason, I'll bet you a lunch that Bush is going to win.

**Jason:** I'll bet you an ice cream if Clinton wins!

*April '93*

*In the following section, Mitchell describes a trip he made to Washington, D.C.*

I was part of the Governmental Affairs Seminar as a participant.... Lots of delegations from ... other chapters of the arc* was there.... The main objective was when we went to the Hill and talked to our congressional leaders ... to support the arc's position.... The arc's position on many of the issues is that they wanted more benefits. They wanted more funding for things....

When I was part of the seminar, there was a lot of meetings breaking down into categories. One category was about health care, one was about long-term care, one was about fetal alcohol syndrome, the other was about the Clinton economic plan and something about the Developmental Disabilities Act. As I was saying, these are the categories they split up.

... When I went on the Hill, me and a couple of other people spoke to [Senators] D'Amato and Moynihan, and [Congressman] McNulty. Let me clarify one thing that I did not spoke to them directly. We spoke to some of their aides who have been working with these congressional leaders. We spoke generally about all these issues which I already raised, and it appeared that we certainly got the message across.

...[They] asked us which certain areas that we are concerned about. I raised the issue about employment because I felt that people with developmental disabilities and mental

---

*Formerly called the National Association for Retarded Citizens

retardation need opportunities to have a job, to work in competitive employment. And I stressed the impact of having
more funding to create more jobs not just for mental retardation and developmental disabilities but generally....

From that point I stated about the film EMPLOY*ABILITY
that was shown. I told them that part of the film is important
for all people and our congressional leaders to look at so that
they know how to start creating new jobs or to find new jobs
for people with developmental disabilities.

EMPLOY*ABILITY is a film that was made by Woolworth
Corporation.... It was their employees' idea.... [It] shows that
people with developmental ... can work and can have the opportunity to work in today's competitive employment. From
my perspective, it makes good business sense to have people
of this kind of nature to work in these ... position[s] because
they have the right to work, to earn money, to make a living of
their own.

And also from my perspective, I feel that when these jobs
are created they should be nondiscriminatory toward mental
and physical disability and developmental disabilities. Because
if it is discriminatory, people will be divided and disgusted,
because in today's society, we want people to work. We want
people to have jobs, to earn money because it's part of the goal
that everyone needs. To have the chance to be successful, to
have a chance to work in the environment where other people
are working.

Now since I am in this film, I feel that I had achieved a
lot.... I can help to deliver this message—that it is important
for people with disabilities can have the same opportunities as
anybody else.

They showed in the film that I was working at a bank in
Summit, New Jersey, as a bulk teller. By working with coins
and taking the train to and from work. James Earl Jones has
narrated this film because he also has a disability because he

stutters. And it also shows that even people who are famous can have a disability as well.

Not only James Earl Jones but also Chris Burke, who we all know because he is star of "Life Goes On." ... What Chris, myself, and Jason—all three of us—have different backgrounds but we do have one thing in common. That is we want support for people with disabilities. We want to see that people with disabilities have a better future ahead of them in every way as possible.

We also want that people to hear what we are trying to say and that is to keep minds open and keep eyes peeled. We, as people with Down syndrome, can make a big difference....

... About six hundred people attended the showing of the film *EMPLOY\*ABILITY* in the Senate Office Building in Washington. A couple of people attended was James Earl Jones and Chris Burke and others. Some of them was congressional leaders and their aides. And there were also people from different organizations for the disabled. It was exciting. It was fun.... It got a lot of good reactions—I was gonna say great! The film will definitely make a difference.

# 12
# Becoming Independent
### "Get Off My Back Please!"

*August '90*

**Mitchell:** One thing I don't like was my mother nagging. "Do you have your wallet? Do you have your keys? Make your bed. Do this, do that." Constantly nagging.... My mother always asking me to take out the garbage. Always on my case, on my back.

**Emily:** If she hadn't reminded you, would you have remembered your keys and your wallet, et cetera?

**Mitchell:** Yes, I always remembered everything.

**Barbara:** That's absolutely true. That's why I stopped nagging you. Mothers have to grow up, too, and let their kids be independent.

**Mitchell:** Mothers and fathers have to learn not to be overprotective.

**Barbara:** Jason, do you think *your* parents are overprotective?

**Jason:** I know my mom has said, "Did you take a shower? Did you brush your teeth? Did you wash your face?" ... As I might say, most parents are just letting their child to be not to be independent. I say that's disrespectful of the child. They're trying to abuse their child. It's called child abuse.

**Emily:** But, Jason, if I didn't remind you, would you remember?

**Jason:** Time to time I forgot—but most of the time I do the things. Sometimes I do the things I forgot but remember the next time. If I forgot to make my bed, I would make my bed the next time on my own. I do the things beforehand that I remember and make my parents feel happy. I would prefer not reminding at all.

**Mitchell:** I would say the same thing—but I'd like to add something else. I'd like to add that parents should not tell their children constantly remind them to do this, do that and also not to be protective as much. If I go out, they should not be worried or protective because I feel hurt if my parents tell me, "Don't forget to call, leave a note." Sometimes I would call just to make sure that *they're* okay and not worrying.

Parents should act their own age because they know that the responsibilities are ours, not theirs. If I do my own responsibilities, and get it done without any problems, I can be independent . . . without somebody telling me what to do every single second of the day. If it's important, leave a little message saying don't forget to—only something very important. Not something idiotic.

**Jason:** Even though it is important, I can do the things that they want me to do or they don't want me to do. If I do the things that is very important for them, then I'll be proud of myself and I like to suggest that to Mitchell. Because some of the parents are just taking it too hard with the kids. Take too much serious turn with the kids. . . .

I never get a chance to be myself. A lot of strange changes inside of me. Like I get to be independent. I start high school. I start to do something important that I can do very well myself. And more math problems and all that stuff. Mentally I'm growing up. I'm getting hair on my legs and my arms. I'm getting to shave now. Now I'm sharing the same songs as

my dad. I changed a lot. It's so strange, ... being independent.
**Mitchell:** Yes. With the experience of going away over the summer, I have proved myself that I can be independent. That I'm very responsible and resourceful.

It's hard for parents to get over the child ... that they're going away. By being away and being independent, it's difficult for the parents to understand because parents need the child there to help and for guidance. There's more to it. The child needs time and space for themselves to succeed and to have a successful life. It's difficult for parents to understand. But I know parents are very supportive and they may or may not agree with the decision. Sometimes their decisions are right.

### July '90

**Mitchell:** I feel that it is important for a person to drive because how are they going to get transportation to jobs, to school? Not only buses, but how are they going to learn for themselves in the future? To be independent? ... I'm not being allowed to drive until a certain age—like twenty-one—because my parents feel you can be trusted and responsible for taking the situation seriously. It's timing.
**Jason:** It's so hard to talk about. Difficult question. I need special skills to drive, to learn easily, so I could take more driving lessons. Sometimes you get ready at a certain age when you're sixteen or eighteen to get ready to drive. You got to study for a couple of years.... You got to get your judgment. You have to obey the same laws as everyone else. Sometimes a child who has Down syndrome can lose his judgment a little because they're not learning as much as we expected.

### August '90

**Jason:** Sometimes it makes me feel upset when people are trying to be nice and saying that we'll see about driving and we'll see how you can get the skills. And I keep telling my parents how much I want a car because there are a lot of reasons why. Some teenagers are good drivers, and each good teenage driver takes their girlfriends out for a date in their car. And I want to be a part of that.

Finally my mom had told me some things that are not good drivers that are causing trouble. "Well, down by Elmsford there's a traffic, a car cutting in line in our road, and that's a crazy driver, especially without a signal." I don't feel I would do that. I think I'm a good driver.

**Emily:** What if it turns out you won't be able to drive because of your Down syndrome?

**Jason:** I'd feel a little bit upset. A lot upset. It's very hard to say it, you know. Because I'm upset. I know some of my parents are teaching me how to be independent. But the question of the driving and how it makes me feel [is] sad. It takes a lot of pain for me learning to be independent, and even if I don't drive then I'm always dependent and take me somewhere.

**Mitchell:** I think I would like to drive so that I could run my own business and to get [what] I need when I'm independent. I do feel driving is important to me so I can have a chance to explore my needs.... Driving may be hard, but I have a feeling that I may succeed at a certain age I would try it and see if it works out or not. If it doesn't work out, I would try another kind of transportation. Like taking a bus or a subway or probably a taxicab. I think I'll be able to do it at a certain time. I'm not studying just yet, but pretty soon I am probably going study how to drive.

*June '91*

**Jason:** Different kinds of traveling—we're not talking about traveling now around the home—means taxis, buses, trains, and planes—

**Mitchell:** How about saying "et cetera" instead of a whole list?

**Jason:** Trains, buses, and taxis, and all that.

We're talking about traveling experiences. Ways to travel. What we're doing now about travel itself.

**Emily:** Mitchell, we know, has had experience traveling by himself on the city bus system.

**Mitchell:** And on the subways with the Summit Travel program with a group.

**Emily:** Jason hasn't done too much alone traveling as yet, but we're starting to work on that. Mitchell, tell us how you learned to use the bus system by yourself.

**Mitchell:** It's very simple to explain. All you have to do is go by the bus stop, give the money, and get onto the bus and get where you're getting to.

**Jason:** But you forgot one more thing before you got to the bus stop. You have to find out what time the bus picks you up and drops you off.

**Mitchell:** It's very easy to tell. For example, when I get home from school, all I do is walk down to the bus stop, wait till it comes, get on the bus. I will just give him the money and go to my job.

**Barbara:** Don't different buses have different numbers?

**Mitchell:** But they go to the same stop. Those particular buses goes to the same stops. Because it's a certain bus number....

It's very easy because I know the sense of direction. The reason it's easy for me because I've had the experience and Jason doesn't have the experience.

It's very easy to recognize the way of transportation-wise. You have to cut to the bone and get to the main part of this. We should basically discuss travel, not transportation. The travel part is being there and having a fun time.

**Jason:** And most important, you have to wear your watch.

**Mitchell:** Jason, I always wear my watch. I've been very responsible, and I know the basics and I know what I need.

**Jason:** I might need to wear a watch. To travel, I need to know when to drop off.

When I travel with Mitchell with the City Lights program, I have to wear a watch because I don't know the route to City Lights. You have to know the route. It's important to travel....

**Mitchell:** I emphasize that traveling is a fun adventure. They must know that it will be tough, but they have to realize it's part of life. It's a part of meeting other people and to make friends with them ... so that down the road they can do things with them. So that they won't be far away and separate that friendship. That friendship is special, so in all, traveling is an aspect to realizing the real world and the importance of independency.

**Jason:** But—you need judgment when you're going to travel because you have to find out and analyze your memory of where you want to go, plan ahead so you can pack your things before you travel. Then go and travel and see your travel schedule. Like a guidebook or something.

**Mitchell:** Jase, that is important ... what you say about making decisions and having judgment about right and wrong.

This all falls into part of living on your own: independence. In order to be independent you have to make decisions, have to be made by yourself. Those decisions have to be made from what is important experience-wise.

**Jason:** Mitchell, who will judge your decisions to see what if it's right or wrong? A person with Down syndrome don't know the difference between right and wrong. They need someone to help them. Have good judgment.

**Mitchell:** They have to discover it themselves.... It's not about other people helping them. They have to benefit making decisions from their own experience. By having experiences, by having a reputation built up by maturity. That maturity will prove the fact that they can be reliable, independent person.

And that's what I'll be doing next year. Because my parents

won't be around to help me make decisions. I'll have to make those decisions by myself....

**Jason:** Communication is important [for traveling] because you can develop pronunciation and vocabulary so they can understand you easily. And speak slowly so they can understand every word. So they can understand of what you're dealing with and your point of traveling where you want to go.

If you want to ask somebody about where you want to go, you have to pronounce slowly.... [It] confuses people at first, but as they get used to it, they start to develop that skill and then they understand you.

**Mitchell:** Communication is important aspect of life because we need to communicate to tell other people how we feel. If we tell them how we feel, they will respect us even more....

**Barbara:** There's another level of this that's very important. Communication provides information. Sometimes when you're traveling, you need different kinds of information.

**Jason:** There's many other kinds of informations — called spoken information, written information, and reading information. You always have to read written directions because when you're traveling if you don't know the spoken, have them help you to write the directions so you can go into that place.

And instructions, too. You have to be instructed. If you don't know the directions, repeat it to yourself. If you're not sure of that, ask questions.

Spoken. You got to know spoken information because if you're doing something that is not in with the spoken information, you may not know what that guy is talking about, so it's a better idea that you should use communication with spoken directions and once you're listening to a tourist guide, and try to remember what he said.

And that is also good for emergency. Emergency is when you get lost someplace. You stay there and then tell someone that is close by where you might go and most important thing is you have to need your ID card.... You ask a cop or a friend that knows you. Or if not, go to a nearest telephone and call to your friend or your family member so he can find your group.

The main thing is to keep up with the group all the time. If you're alone and you get lost, you go to a nearest telephone, call up a family member to help you.... That city might be a big city. You ask for a friend or a family member or a police officer. Or a train operator.

**Mitchell:** There's not always a train operator there. There are people around you can ask for instructions. If you're lost it may not be as easy, but if you do, there's always maps around you can look at.

**Barbara:** So you can see how important it is that you're able to communicate, that you use the skills you've developed, that people understand you when you speak.

**Mitchell:** That why we have speech and language because if we have that, we are able to use all our connections . . . so that we can understand . . . and taking that further, the next step forward. Outside in the real world.

*May '92*

**Mitchell:** From my perspective that driving may be important to a person, but it takes a person the time to learn how to drive. It is one of those unrealistic things when you're in your teenage. It would be unrealistic if you're a teenager. But if you're a young adult like my age, like twenty-one or sometime down the road would be more realistic. Because then you will have the understanding why it is important that you want to learn how to drive a car. Someday I do wish I would like to drive a car, but it will take some time for me to learn the appropriate skills.... I have a feeling that I can learn.

**Jason:** It takes some time because you have to study the manual and practice until you get your skills down pat. And then you go to the DMV to get your written test. That's a little bit hard, but you feel you can learn. And the day of your written test, you get that out of the way and then you start to go on the road to do your driving test. It takes about four driving tests until you get your license. If you pass all four, you have your own license and you can drive. Like I said earlier, step by step.

**Barbara:** Why do you think that your parents are reluctant to have you learn how to drive?

**Mitchell:** Because they are worried about the safety of their child. They are worried they will be rejected if they do not pass the test or the examination. But on the most part, parents sometimes are a little bit too overprotective regarding the decision of the child who wants to learn how to drive a car.

**Barbara:** When you had a discussion with Dad about driving—

**Mitchell:** He was concerned that I would not understand that it would take a while for me to learn to be able to take on such responsibility because sometimes when my father relies on me for certain things, he feels that certain things I can make a good decision. Regarding driving, he might think my decision is not appropriate at this stage.

**Jason:** ...Sometimes my mom is a little bit worried because I may go out to a road that has crazy drivers and you may feel that you have an accident. If your mom thinks and takes a look in your car and there's a dent in it, there's a problem. More serious than a dent is you might get killed. That's very serious. That is worth worrying about, getting killed.

**Mitchell:** Two very important episodes on "Life Goes On" regarding Tyler that he was in a car accident and he dies because he was under the influence of alcohol. Part of this has to do with the decision—what the person can learn. Most people feel they know what is right and wrong...but they need to [be] pointed out to the right direction.

When I saw those two episodes of "Life Goes On," it captured a certain emotion regarding having a person who is disabled to drive like other people do. It's a very difficult step for a person with Down syndrome to take. Your disability can have some effect on learning how to drive. I feel that may come up. . . .

**Jason:** It's very hard to take a test because of your disability. For driving you have to be extremely careful because that's the pain . . . like in the news, saying a disabled person died in a car crash. You have to be extremely careful how you drive.

**Mitchell:** Andrea Friedman, who is now on "Life Goes On," in the one episode when she and Drew got into that crash and Corky finds out that she was driving a car, it made him feel that he wanted to learn to drive himself.

In some cases a person who is disabled can be able to learn how to drive, but it may take a while. But some restrictions are made like, for example, it takes a long time of study and preparation to take those examinations. But watching that show really recaps a very important part in that driving may be important to a person who has Down syndrome. But Andrea Friedman made an important decision with some support from her parents. She made a very committed decision, which a person with Down syndrome should do about taking that responsibility.

*March '92*

*The following sections were written by Jason.*

Dear friends, adults, teachers, and parents,

This is Jason Kingsley. I am utterly alone and stressfully upset.

I will tell you why. I know I am learning about school and life, but I have a difficulty to learn things. Now I understand a lot of stuff. Can you let me be on my own and in the future? You will have to let go of me. I'm not a kid and a teenager. Seventeen years I'm dying to be a man. "Get off my back please!" Even though I am deciding things now, I want to <u>be myself</u>

<u>alone</u>. It's not easy but this is the way it is. I'm sorry to make you upset but let me to be free.

> Thank you,
> Jason Kingsley

Here is my nightly schedule. I go home, relax, have a snack, do homework, wait for Dad, have dinner (no dessert), relax, watch a movie, shower or a shampoo, and then sleep.

Here is my hard and "<u>difficult problem</u>": life. Sometimes I have conflict between everything I do. I'm right between a kid or a man. I'm right between what my mom wants and what my dad wants. Panic, tragedy. Where my life is going to.

I have many hard "pressure problem" problems that covers all of my life. I always "<u>forget</u>" everything. I lose my mind a lot. My mind splits open when I forgot things even when my teachers want me to remember, but I can't remember.

I am always trying hard to do best I can.

### August '92

*The following sections were written by Mitchell.*

My first job I got at Jespy is a volunteer job at the Assemblywoman Maureen Ogden's. I work in her office as a clerical aide. Part of my job is to file and to open the mail and to stamp them. I also stamp booklets to be put out in the office. I take the train to work in Milburn where Maureen Ogden's office is located. I work in the office for a couple of hours.

Since December, I am working at Summit Trust as a bulk teller. I take the train to Summit to the bank where I work. Part of my job at Summit Trust is to sort coins, rebagging, and to write the ticket that goes on the bag of coins. I also do the microfilming batches of checks and sometimes I help my supervisor Eileen by bringing the money to the drive-up. My supervisor Eileen is a bank teller. She takes the money from the customers....

I have a second job and it is part time. I work at Pizza Hut on Tuesdays and Fridays. I take the Jespy van to work and coming back from work. My responsibilities at the job are [to] prep garlic bread and clean off and refill the salad bar. Then I became the manager of the dishwasher. So far this is what I've done. I'm getting five dollars and five cents an hour. I'm having a fun time working there. The people who I work with are very nice to me and they feel very comfortable with me working there.

### Spring '92

*The following section was written by Jason.*

I have a job in the Library four days a week. The rest of the days...I go to Speech. In the Library I help out like filing, putting books in order, cleaning TV sets and I do lots of stuff.

I also work on Saturday mornings. I work for Frank and Carl's Dry Cleaners in Chappaqua.... I made $5.00 but I got a $2.00 raise so now I make $7.00. I work for two hours—9:00 to 11:00. I put guards on hangers. The guards are for when you hang up the clothes on the hanger, you won't get a wrinkle. I have worked there for two years. I work with other guys like Omar who does the pressing, Denise who is a girl who also does pressing, Tino, Carl, Mike, and Frank. They are nice. They play my favorite station WNEW-AM 1130. I sing along there.

As when I was in high school, I make $12.00 of allowance to pay for my lunch and my train fare. And now I use my half-fare transit card for when I go to my train, I pay half price. Whatever is left over I can save for my savings. I bought myself a VCR from my savings. It is very hard to save up the money for my car because a car is very expensive.

### March '93

**Jason:** I'm eighteen years old and this is the way I feel about being independent.... I feel a little bit on the happy side, I say about 70 percent...and 30 percent sad.

I'm always taking pride of being independent. Because it makes me feel like a mature man. I feel independent on social, economically on dates (that means spending money on movies and that stuff), decisions, making the right decisions work.

There is family problems that I would like to talk about in independence—that I want my parents to get off my back....

I know they're very proud of me being independent. But they're not doing their job of letting me making decisions. This morning is one.... I don't want my dad to tell me that I need to read. I have books in my room. It's my room.... Dad said that even though I'm making decisions, I have to read anyway and that's not right. Because I want to make the decisions on reading, too. That's why I need my dad to get off my back.

...If I feel that I wanted to read, I'm going to read. But...I can do some other things like watching TV, like listen to my stereo or playing piano or any other thing that keeps me productively and having fun.

**Emily:** Do you know why Dad wants you to do some reading?

**Jason:** Because he wants me to expand my brain. I don't want to expand my brain *too* much. I really need some space and have fun....

**Emily:** What about living independently—in an apartment or house or getting married? Are you ready for that yet? To leave us and live on your own? Do you think you would miss us?

**Jason:** At some point I would miss my mom and dad because I love them. They're so happy for me. They're also very proud of my independence. But I don't really miss them *that* much. That's because I am doing some very independent things.

I would like to visit them and probably have some time to relive my past if I wanted to. We could talk about the old days. I can still do the things I can do in my apartment and still have time to visit with them and have fun.

I need also some help on transportation in the future. I'm not going to get to the train or the bus that often. I might take a taxi even though it's expensive. But I need some training on studying the driver's manual and looking forward to buy a nice red Saab turbo black-top-down convertible — exciting and amusing by boys and sexy to girls. There are some places the bus don't go or the train don't go, so why not get a car?!

**Emily:** And what happens if that doesn't happen? If you're not able to get a car or a driver's license?

**Jason:** I'll still get some more training on it. I'll still go on local transportation like bus or train or taxi. But when I am comfortable of driving a car, I'll be happy to.

*January '93*

**Emily:** Today Jason and I were talking about wouldn't it be nice if you could just automatically become independent. And I said there were a lot of things to learn before you can be totally independent.

**Mitchell:** To me, to put it into perspective, you have to think that things do not happen overnight. It takes time. In my case, I do think that I know what I want to do. It's difficult processing that. I do want to live fully independently, without anyone looking over me all the time.

**Jason:** ... That's what I want to do, too. I didn't want to be independent automatically, but what I'm saying about automatically means to me means that I can teach and learn myself about what kind of skills I took in my past and see if I can do better. Do new things I've never been doing before. Do new steps.

I can do it myself without being taught ... because there are some things that I want to do for myself. Not only for my family to help me because I want to be happy and have some fun and be independent. To be by myself.

**Mitchell:** Part of my problem is most of the time I know what I want to do. Sometimes I think that I'm a big shot. What I meant was most of the time that I know what I'm doing ... but sometimes — I don't explain to other people that I don't understand what I'm doing. Most of the time I tell them, "I know how to do this. I can do this on my own." But sometimes I *can't* do it on my own, because certain things I need help with. And people could help me to understand that it's something I need to work on.

Sometimes I think that in a certain category we're considered as experts. Sometimes I think that even though I know a lot of things, sometimes I feel that I can take control over certain situations. When someone tells me you're not in position to state your view about it or state your solution to the problem. Sometimes, with my reputation, the way I built it, that I use my rights as an issue....

**Jason:** You're going back for people to help you. You work your life to be independent with no help, ... and now you're coming back to where people have to help you and that's not right.

**Emily:** Can you see that there some areas where *you* need help, Jason?

**Jason:** No. I can do *everything*, so long as I learn them. I can take one step easy into a hard thing. Like we did in transportation. I learned how to do it myself. First I went on the train with you. Then we went in separate seats. Then you waited at the other station. Now I can do it independently all by myself. I want to do it in little steps up to a difficult thing to do. To be independent with no other people to help. Because you have fun and you like to have no help.

**Emily:** Are there *any* things you need help with?

**Jason:** No. Only transportation.

**Mitchell:** How about your social skills? Between you and me, both of us have problems the way we socialize with other people. Do you think that's one of the skills you need to work on?

**Jason:** Now I got a little more experience with social skills, talking to people. It's like I'm always saying, once you do it, the less help you can get. I got a lot of help in the beginning from my social life. But now I'm coming a long way. I'm getting too far advanced of that. Now I can socialize with other people. Because I learned a lot from other people. And now I'm fully grown up to do things for myself even though people are still helping me.

Part of it . . . for me, I need to do more things with other people, like going out, even to a movie or to a park or for dinner or something like that. Going out, doing things with others, getting into a relationship. . . .

Part of being friends is doing things with other people. I have been making friends but I haven't been going out and doing things with them. . . . The point I'm trying to make here is that I do want to go out and do things with others so that I could have some experience of doing those kinds of things which I've never done before at all.

**Emily:** How do you think you will improve that situation?

**Mitchell:** By approaching an individual and asking them if they want to do something with me for a day off or a couple of hours. This really is the only issue that I really need to work on with the Jespy program. The other issues I can handle on my own without any problems. They're helping me by realizing that I have to improve by making sure I'm doing things with others, not just sitting around watching TV all the time.

**Jason:** Some of the ways that I can be with other people is by letting my parents know where I'm supposed to be. . . . If I want to be with that person I'm talking to at the phone, if I want to go to the movies with them, I have to let my mom know. . . .

**Mitchell:** Part of being respectful is letting your parents know, or leave a note or a phone call when you'll be back. It's important to put into perspective that exactly what you plan doing.

Part of a parent's perspective is they want to be comfortable, not to be worried about what you're doing. Many people are very sadistic, very sick, and may do something to you. Parents may be worried about what might happen to you. That's why there should be lots of communication between you and parents about what you're doing. You should talk this out.

**Jason:** Let me go back to what I said before. It's true that I have to let my parents know where I am and when I'm coming back. It's very important. I know that. But I'm fully independent to tell my parents. I didn't want my mom to force me to tell her about where am I going and when I am coming back.

**Mitchell:** You should tell her. Not ask her permission. You don't need to ask her permission. You just need to tell her, to give her some indication of what you're doing.

**Jason:** If I do that, I'm fully independent to talk to her...of going someplace and coming back.

**Mitchell:** Jason, let me tell you something about my two sisters. If they want to go out with their friends, they would be kind or respectful by calling or leave a note of some indication of when they're leaving or when they're coming back. They would say, "Hi, I'm going out with my friends. I will be back at this time or this time." That would give an indication that they left a notice of their plans and when they're coming back so our parents will not be worried about what they're doing. You need to be respectful to your parents. It's part of being an individual.

**Jason:** How independent are you about asking parents' permission or telling people you're going someplace? If you are independent you have no trouble.

**Mitchell:** I'm talking about being independent. I'm talking about doing what you know is best. Just trying to make the effort. It's part of being respectful. That's what it's about.

**Jason:** It's a mixture of independence.... You want to be independent for all your life for each basic step. Here's a situation. If I said, "Hi, I'm going someplace." Knowing when to get help, when to ask if you want to go out someplace. To clarify this, let's say if you're all alone with nothing to do and you want to go someplace with your friend, would you be independent and tell your mom about that you're going someplace with that person? I would be independent by telling my mom where I'm going and when I'm coming back. Then I do what you say about being respectful and showing some signs and then I'm fully more independent. As my dad says, I'm learning every day. I'm learning some new things.

**Mitchell:** Everyone is learning new things all the time. I don't want to get into a debate here. The important thing to realize, even if you're living independently, you need to make decisions on your own. Parents want you to make decisions by yourself. Just courtesy and respect is all they ask for.

**Jason:** It's a complicated thing. You want to do *that* independently yourself, too.

**Mitchell:** No, it's not a complicated issue at all. From my perspective, parents are considered to have some notice.

**Barbara:** I think even if you're living away from your parents, you still have to be thoughtful of the other people you're living with who care about you. If you're doing something with a friend, let the people know so they won't worry about you, that's all.

It brings out a very good issue for anybody as a young adult.... Transportation problems can really restrict you a lot in terms of how independent you can be, how much you can socialize with other people, where you can work, how you get there. Is that an issue for you?

**Emily:** Jason, if you wanted to take Ellen out to dinner and a movie, how would you do it?

**Jason:** How about the parents?

**Barbara:** That's the point! In that situation, you must depend on the parents to get you where you want to go.

**Jason:** How about Ellen's parents?

**Barbara:** Fine, but you'll need to ask *somebody* for help.

**Jason:** Then *she* won't be independent.

**Mitchell:** Talking to my father about driving, I asked him if I could have a car. Some things are restricted because of the way I behave myself. He's worried about the kind of control I have or the kind of temper I have. Sometimes I do some things on impulses.

To me, I do want to drive, but it's difficult for me to have the skills to drive. My father doesn't see me driving until a certain age. Dad, he sees me driving at twenty-three, which is next year, but I think that's not going to happen. I don't think I'm gonna have the skills by twenty-three or twenty-four. Or at all.

There will be other methods of transportation. I don't think I will ever get those skills. It's difficult for me to face, but I'm learning to accept the fact that I may not be able to do some things that my sisters are doing. Which is a main fact which I will understand.

Some things that my disability can or cannot do. I can't force myself. The important thing is I realize that there are other advantages that I have like, for example, public transportation....

**Jason:** If you're taking the driver's ed course, there are people that can teach you the skills you need to drive.... Once I get into the driver's ed course, for me to try, and if that didn't work out, I might accept that I can use public transportation.

**Mitchell:** On the show of "Life Goes On," Andrea Friedman [has Down syndrome and] she is independent in real life. She has a car and she is driving. Some people are committed to drive and some people are not.

Sometimes [a person] with a disability is restricted from certain things.... Between me and Jason that I don't think it would be quite wise for us to drive now because we don't have the skills for it. You need to have the commitment to do so and be able to do that throughout your life.

For Andrea, she is learning how to drive with the help of her parents, which helps her a lot to get places where she wants to go. The important thing is that our disability restricts us to certain skills. This is one of the things. Driving is a big step. It's something many people want to do. I think part of a person's disability has to do with this. Certain things are restricted and certain things are not.

**Jason:** You may be not ready to drive, but you're old enough to accept to take any other public transportation....

I don't want to talk about this. It's too painful to talk about.

**Mitchell:** I think Jason should talk about it. It's important for people to know what his feelings are concerning his fears about his disability regarding if he wants to drive or not. I think he should confront it.

**Jason:** Sometimes I may do that. I have to be flexible and be comfortable first. Before you confront your feelings, you don't want to be angry and pressured by confronting your feelings. You can't fight your feelings, but you can overcome it by accepting the fact that some areas can restrict you from driving.

**Mitchell:** The point I'm making about your feelings, I cannot judge your feelings, but I think the people really want to know how do you really feel about driving. Is it something you really want to do? What are your feelings about it?

**Jason:** I think it might be too risky for me. Both driving and confronting my feelings. You don't want to be confronting your feelings if you're depressed.... You want to be calmed down first and then confront your feelings. I gotta be calm. I gotta be flexible. I gotta confront my feelings, but I have to calm down first.

**Emily:** Are you disappointed that you may not drive?

**Mitchell:** I'm not really that quite disappointed because I expected this to happen because generally that's the way I feel. I don't feel it's that important to me at this time. I can wait till the time comes or whenever....

When the time comes, I'll make the decision.

# 13
# Our Future Plans

## "It's the End of a Story, but a New Chapter in Our Book"

*August '90*

*Mitchell is about to enter his final year of high school. These are his future plans:*

**Mitchell:** [I am] planning on college, planning on being independent. I've been looking at colleges like New York Institute of Technology.... It's the same [kind of] program that I'm in now.... It's more harder and you take more time for me to study.... It would take a while to understand and to know the information. I may need some extra help.

College could be difficult, but it could be fun. One would be, you're without your family.... Two, you're independent. Three, I have to take responsibility for myself. And the hardest part to make the right decisions and the right judgment.

I feel I will study more about government and politics. How the government works and how my skills will get better. My reading skills and writing skills.

[After college], I probably would get a job working in a government office and to learn the same skills and do what I'm doing now in Assemblyman George Pataki's office in Peekskill.

I work one day a week [there], after school. When I get there, I do the mail, filing, and also straighten things out in the office. I also send things out to the mail. I also cut out articles from the newspapers to put on file. Articles that are in the district. This is a voluntary job. For interning. When George Pataki asked me to go to Albany with him, he took me on the floor of the assembly. He made a nice introduction about me, and then everyone applauded.

I also got my picture taken with Assemblyman George Pataki and another assemblyman. And I also saw a senator, Senator Nick Spano. And I got my picture taken with him.

This is in influencing my future goals, where I'm going after college. One of the things after college which I plan doing is working in the White House. In discussion with the president of the U.S., what other acts that we could put into law for people with disabilities.

*Jason is about to enter his first year of high school. These are his future plans:*

**Jason:** Finish education—meaning finish all four years of high school...get a career, ends at sixty-five, then retire and go to another career.

**Emily:** What kind of career?

**Jason:** A teacher's aide. Well, I gotta go back to my old school and teach the seventh or eighth graders science, English, French, Spanish, and speech. I have fifth period off for lunch. Not for little kids. I want to work with bigger kids.... It's an easy career.

**Emily:** What kind of things do you have to do in that career?

**Jason:** Eye contact, shake hands, be responsible, don't be late, be on time, keep the right clothes on, do your work well, do your work in a faster pace.

**Emily:** Why do you want that job?

**Jason:** So I can teach some kids how to do reading and business letters like I do. Also showing people what I have learned from junior high school that I can teach the kids.

**Mitchell:** You say you want to be a teacher's aide. Would that be difficult for you for having a disability?

**Jason:** No, it doesn't affect my disability at all. That's the way it is and I can teach people some things that I feel.

**Mitchell:** From my point of view, I seriously think it might be affected by the disability because of a person's speech.... The other students or the teacher might not understand what the aide is trying to say. It won't be as clear as possible. From my experience, people had a hard time understanding me because of my speech.

**Jason:** I have the best speech in the world.... I don't think people can't understand what I'm saying. I have very good speech. I get speech therapy....

**Mitchell:** From my point of view, the important thing is not that they don't understand you, it could help you project, help you to speak better. Then in the future, more people could understand you much better if you have good fluency in order to express yourself. Like for example if I were going to have an interview for college, I should speak more clear so they can understand the information I'd tell them so that they know what kind of strong and what kind of reason I have....

*February '91*

**Emily:** You say, "I want to have a future of my own." I'd like to hear about how you imagine that future to be. How do you picture yourself, let's say, ten or fifteen years from now?

**Mitchell:** I would like to run for president of the United States....

**Emily:** How do you feel the American public would respond to a person with a disability, a person with Down syndrome, running for president of the United States?

**Mitchell:** I think they would understand the views. They basically understand the consequences because some cases when parents have their children who has a disability, they would look up to the person who's running for president and who will make the world a safer place.

I feel it would take a lot of responsibility to be president. The responsibilities the president should make should be taken seriously, and a person with a disability should be able to make those decisions. Those decisions will be tough to make but you understand what's going on because you have an understanding of the past presidents. For myself, for example, I understand what's going on in the world because I keep up with the news and what's going on in the world. That's why I believe I can make a really good president. Because I share the views with my fellow citizens.

**Emily:** Do you think you could win?

**Mitchell:** I have reason to believe I will win—because with my friendships and relationships with people I have, they have an understanding of people with disabilities, and take responsibilities seriously and to set priorities straight. And one of the parts have to do with the motivation and the organizing.

**Barbara:** Jason, it's your turn. How do you imagine your life ten to fifteen years from now? What will you be doing?

**Jason:** Well, there's two jobs that I should do. One, I have to stick with my career as a teacher's aide because that's my business so I can support my wife and my children.

I may be a news forecaster. Able to think about the weather or traffic. Well in traffic, I can say about the Throgs Neck Bridge some of the cars are blocked up because of road construction. And about the weather: in the Metropolitan Area it might be quite breezy and cold out and it looks like it might get warm again later in the week. High in the upper fifties. And for the sports, the Rangers beat the Devils 3 to 2. It was a tie game and then they made a beautiful shot to win it. Let's see the stock market close and the gold prices. And the winning lottery numbers. And the news.

I would like to do more acting, but I've got to tell my parents some shows I'd like to be in. Not only TV shows but Broadway shows. I'd like to act in Broadway shows. I'd be great as Herbie in *Gypsy*. I'd be great as Don Lockwood in *Singin' in the Rain*. I'd like to do musicals, speaking lines, singing lines, and probably some acting lines in different parts.

### April '91

**Barbara:** Mitchell, you are now preparing for your graduation from high school in June. Why do you think they call the graduation ceremonies a "commencement," or a beginning?
**Jason:** I think it's the beginning of your future life.
**Mitchell:** It is also the end of a story, but it is a new chapter in your book.

What begins is after the graduation it is a new story. It's a new story, a new chapter entitled "The Future and the Goals That I Am Planning for the Future Ahead."

I see in my future realistically by being able to work in government, in an office, being able to continue my skills by joining a residence program down in South Orange, New Jersey, where I have most of my friends . . . and they will give me some knowledge that I achieved certain skills already, but I need to practice more of these skills to continue on the path to the future. Now I am on a waiting list until an apartment is open and when I am accepted to move in, I am able to continue on with my future. This is a step which is important to continue on instead of going ahead and getting a job right away.

When an apartment opens up, then I am able to move into the apartment with four or five other people and I get to share the apartment with them. Also there are certain chores that have to be done and each person does a certain chore each day, such as cooking, cleaning, shopping. . . .

And the other part is to be able to hold your money and to be able to use a budget that is useful to do all I want. The other part with the jobs I'd be involved in is the people who are in charge of the program go out and find a job the person is interested in from the interview. And after they find the jobs, they will tell the person that they found a job that is fit for you and you go into that job and get started. And the other part is that you get paid for the job, for my knowledge. And with the transportation, they may have a van or a bus to take you to the job where the place is located.

After work, they do certain activities going on. They may have dances, they will go to basketball games or down in city hall and they also probably go to wrestling matches down in New York. They take a van or a bus to New York City to get you to these events. And also there is a synagogue nearby that they have Saturday morning services to attend.

**Jason:** I think having an apartment and job is for you to decide before you graduate from high school. You may decide to go to college for your career to decide what you're doing. Like my career is a teacher's aide. First of all you've got to get the skills to learn about teaching. You have to go to college for four years. Your wave of the future will be to go back to your own house to see how well you've grown up, how smart you are, how caring and loving. Then at that time you decide to go to your apartment. Unless you've got your skills of your career down pat and then you start to go to your career. You can go to career school which is called a college.

**Mitchell:** Jase, it seems to me that you're jumping the gun. Because I know that people in special education and who are disabled, it is not easy for a person who has Down syndrome to go to college because it is not easy for them to be accepted. It is more difficult with the courses. It is much harder for them to handle the concepts.

**Jason:** But not experts like us.

**Mitchell:** I'm talking about the students who are trying to enter those schools. The way I feel is instead of going to college it's better to look for the opportunities where the people can help you, people with disabilities, help you to live on your own...instead of go[ing] to college. To know how important it is to be able to learn...to live on your own, because the concept is that it is difficult for a person with a disability or a person who has Down syndrome.... It is tougher for them to know what's going on. And it is much easier for them to be in a vocational program where there are people there to help you understand to live on your own instead of college. College is much harder.

**Barbara:** This is very important. You know that within the last six months since you have been getting together, you have heard Mitchell talk about the idea of going to college. Now, all of a sudden, you're hearing him say he's decided *not* to go to college but to go to another program to learn to live and work on his own, with other people who have disabilities.

**Mitchell:** The reason why I decided not to go to college because I feel it would be more difficult and tougher and the courses would be harder, too. Like math, science, all those courses that I'd take, like I took already in high school. I don't want to repeat taking the courses again because I believe the strength of the course would be too complicated and too confusing to understand.

...I feel that I do not want to repeat courses again and the pressure on me to do it again without the help from my parents or my sisters who are not going to be there and the program would be too complex to be able to understand.

*March '93*

**Emily:** Jason, what happens after graduation from Lakeland? There are three possibilities: One is go to work, get a job right away. Two is go to college. Three is go into an independence training program in a transitional apartment like Mitchell is doing at Jespy House.

**Jason:** I would like to have a mixture of one, two, and three. That means college of the field of work and training on independence.... I'm looking forward to that. Here's a question: In what schools, or what colleges, would they have a mixture of work experience and introduction to independence?

**Emily:** There are several schools that offer that kind of program. I have literature from some of them, and I am continuing to send away for more. We will get into that very soon.

**Jason:** What are the names of the schools that you look into for work experience and independence?

**Emily:** One is the school on Long Island we visited—New York Institute of Technology. They have a program called VIP—Vocational Independence Program—that includes college classes plus work experience plus independent living in a college dorm. Another one is called the Threshold Program at Lesley College and that's up in Cambridge, Massachusetts, near Harvard. NYU has a para-educator program in New York City. And there are others, too.

**Jason:** That's very nice. And not only about the issues I talked about earlier but also social—like being with friends. I need part work and part social and part fun.

**Emily:** That's exactly what college is supposed to be.

**Jason:** And not only that, it's part of being alone sometimes. Alone to have fun and alone to have work. Like you can have your own work experience with no one except you to be dependent on.

So I make my own expectations. I have high expectations of myself. I expect to get a good job. Good training...good apartment, good wife, good social life, and good everything.

### March '93

*Mitchell has been at Jespy a year and a half and is now ready to consider what comes next.*

**Barbara:** Mitchell, let's explore what it is you're trying to accomplish. If you think about your everyday life, what are some of the things you'd like to be able to do—*wherever* you might live?

**Mitchell:** The first thing is to have a job. Which is in my furthest attention. Earlier on we were discussing all the possibilities, and to some degree that my interest is very important in politics and government. What I was thinking of probably was having one job — like working in an office complex — the other one probably in a major corporation. Even though I'm now working in a bank, which is a major corporation, I'd prefer to be in government.

**Barbara:** What kinds of things are part of the job you'd want?

**Mitchell:** The first thing is to do, instead of sitting at a desk all day, I'd rather go out and go to meetings or meet with clients, like helping people out. In government, because I feel that I am good — I have good ideas in the field. I want to meet people.

The main key is to be productive.... I don't want to be in one place. I want to move around.

What bothers me the most, whenever I have a job, I feel uncomfortable with a job coach. Because usually when a job coach comes in, he or she checks how I'm doing or talks to my supervisors about what's the status, see how I'm doing and how things are going on.

I have no problems with having a supervisor making sure that I'm doing what I'm supposed to be at all times. With a supervisor, I can be more professional and take things more seriously than a job coach. Because it doesn't create any attention to me when I'm busy working on something and when I'm not.

**Jack:** A realistic goal would be to be an assistant to your supervisor. If you're going to be assisting a supervisor or a manager, what kinds of things would you like to do during the day?

**Mitchell:** By running around doing things for my supervisors or my fellow employees. And the other thing is to be involved in meetings because I feel I do have strong intentions and good ideas and suggestions, so I feel my input will be important to my supervisors.

**Jack:** Do you think you're ready to have your own place to live?

**Mitchell:** I can do my own laundry and I can cook. I can take care about my personal hygiene very well. Shopping I have no problems with. That I can handle. Cleaning I can do.

**Barbara:** Would you want to live entirely by yourself or with other people—but with privacy?

**Mitchell:** At the present time, I'd like to live on my own. If I decided, on down the road, that I want to have a roommate, I'll decide then.

First I'd like to have an apartment by myself. Then later, if the time is right, I would like other people to move in with me. When I get settled in first and get comfortable, and know what I'm doing, then I'll be relaxed and won't have any stressed by having other people to live with at the same time. But I'd like it to be my choice....

I do have some experience of being in a single apartment. Right now I have a roommate. He's nice and everything...but now I feel the time is right now...to begin to have my own privacy. To have a single room and then have a single apartment.

**Mitchell:** I'd like to move out into the community....

**Barbara:** How would you like to participate in the community to make your life good?

**Mitchell:** I could join...a committee, like a Republican committee—Republican or Democrat, it doesn't matter—a political committee.

I would want a social program—like for example, sports, going to ball games, sporting events, being involved in services in a synagogue.... There's a lot of things: shopping, going to a mall (I do that all the time), dates, seeing my family, my siblings, doing things with my friends, visit family friends....

**Barbara:** What kinds of things could you make a valuable contribution to in the community?

**Mitchell:** Political kind of things, that's where my interest is. The other things I just said are for social.

...Major importance is to help people with disabilities. Being involved in family support like what Mommy and Emily are doing. That's really important to me. Being an advocate, speaking out, talking to other people with disabilities, seeing what they have to say, speaking to new families. I do want to have a major contribution toward this.

**Barbara:** Now, one of the things that's still a little difficult is budgeting your money. If you were living on your own, how would you get assistance on some of the things you still need some help with?

**Mitchell:** I would go to one of you and I could contact one of you, and you could assist me. My family.

**Barbara:** Would you also be open to getting support from someone coming to visit you? Let's say once every two weeks—like a counselor, a case manager, or a service coordinator—to make sure you don't have questions about that.

**Mitchell:** I think that would be very helpful to me.

**Barbara:** Let's talk now about what kinds of decisions in your everyday life you would like to make for yourself.

**Mitchell:** Where I work, where I live, what I do every day... who I would see without permission from anyone, if people want to see me to make an appointment with me so they don't come at all different times, how I should spend my money, with some consulting....

**Barbara:** You basically want to make all your choices by yourself but get some input from—who?

**Mitchell:** My family, or a counselor, or a lawyer. Gotta have a lawyer....

**Jack:** I want you to think of the next step. You've said you might want to live in Albany or Washington and pursue some kind of government career. When we talk about the next step, we're not ignoring the fact that you want to get to Albany or Washington. In my opinion, I don't think you're ready for that much independence yet.

Let's list your goals and see how they would work in New Jersey and how they would work in Westchester.

**Barbara:** The first thing you said was being part of a political committee. Where's the greater likelihood of your doing that—New Jersey or Westchester?

**Mitchell:** Westchester—because we have a lot of contacts. My *own* contacts. It would be easier to do in Westchester.

**Barbara:** Okay. Now how about some of the synagogue activities?

**Mitchell:** That's in Westchester. I have to say that point blank....

I have more friends in New Jersey than in Westchester.... If I live in New Jersey, I have no problems getting to social or sporting events going on. But if I live in Westchester, I would have a problem.

**Jack:** If it comes out better to live in Westchester, what are you going to do about friends?

**Mitchell:** I will find people to do things with.

**Barbara:** What are some of the ways to find people?

**Mitchell:** Ask them to have dinner or lunch or go to a movie.... Being involved in programs. Through jobs.

**Jack:** Is it possible to accomplish your social life in Westchester?

**Mitchell:** It's a possibility, but I'd give the edge to New Jersey. I feel New Jersey is more established right now. But if I'm in Westchester, you'd be looking in on me to see how I'm doing. I won't want to rely on both of you for many things.

**Jack:** We don't want you to rely on us, either. We want you to be independent. We'll just be there to help you as you need us to. You would have to trust that we wouldn't be constantly interfering in your life.

**Mitchell:** That's right. Is it the same with Leah and Stephanie?

**Barbara:** Exactly.

**Mitchell:** Leah? In what ways?

**Leah:** I have to trust that they are not going to let themselves interfere in my new independence. But it's also nice to know that I can call them and they're close enough. I don't know if you remember, but I was thinking about going to school far away. The idea of them being able to drive up to school quickly made a big difference.

**Mitchell:** I feel the same way. If I'm living in New Jersey, they could come down or I could come up once in a while.

**Leah:** If you live close by to home, do you think you could trust them to keep their distance? Do you trust them to know you need your independence?

**Mitchell:** I can trust them if they can trust me.

**Leah:** If you have a mutual trust going, maybe it could work out.

**Barbara:** Okay, here's a big one. Jobs. What are the job opportunities in New Jersey in terms of what you want to do—and the job opportunities in Westchester? How did you get the Pizza Hut job?

**Mitchell:** I did that. I got that [idea] myself. And the bank job was from connections...with people like Randy Williams, who helped me prepare for the interview.

**Jack:** What about getting jobs in Westchester?

**Mitchell:** We have more connections to know what jobs are available here in Westchester than in New Jersey.

**Barbara:** Whose connections?

**Mitchell:** Yours? [*looks at Barbara*]

**Barbara:** No.

**Mitchell:** Yours? [*looks at Jack*]

**Jack:** No.

**Mitchell:** Mine. My own.

**Barbara:** Well, there are family connections, as well as your own connections that you've made with people in Westchester. In terms of finding out about jobs and getting involved in political committees and other activities in the community, who has the contacts?

**Mitchell:** We do. Here in Westchester.

**Barbara:** Why is that?

**Mitchell:** Because I know more people here and that I know how to contact them.

**Jack:** On paper it sounds like there are more advantages to moving back to Westchester, but you sound, well, resigned — but not too sure about it. I'm watching your face and you're saying, "Yeah, I guess it's the best for me." But you don't seem excited about it. What's the problem?

**Mitchell:** It seems to me that you *want* me to be here instead of New Jersey, because you think I'm more secure knowing that I'm always here, being close by.

To a certain degree I want to be on my own independently. Sometimes you don't let me do that because sometimes I'm not always consistent with the decisions I make.

I don't feel as independent here.

**Barbara:** You don't think we would allow you to be independent. Is that your one big problem with this?

**Mitchell:** Yes.

**Barbara:** If we *guaranteed* you that we'd give you the chance to be as independent as possible, would that make you feel better?

**Mitchell:** Yes....

In the spring I'd like to move back *here*.

**Jack:** Look at the bright side. Back here, Grandpa will be around and you can cook for him a lot. You can invite people for dinner.

**Mitchell:** We could have Passover at my place....

I want to be in the community knowing who I know. Grandpa's here. I can go out and do shopping with Grandpa. And I could work [weekends] at the Terrace with Dad. And go skiing. And go to the lake. All the fun things I've been missing out.

**Jack:** And we promise to keep our distance.

**Barbara:** Right. We only want grown-up children now. Now, what are some of the things we could explore to make this happen?

**Mitchell:** We have to find a place for me to live in. Hey, when are those people moving out next door?

**Jack:** Sometime during the summer.

**Mitchell:** Then in the summer I could move into the house next door! Then we could keep our distance.... I could live here ... but when those people move out, I could move into the house next door.

**Barbara:** What would you need to do to get the house next door ready to move into?

**Mitchell:** Just move my stuff in. Plus the rent and stuff. The money.... I'd have to find a job.

**Jack:** Do you think you could afford the whole rent on the whole house yourself?

**Mitchell:** How much is the rent?

**Jack:** More than you can afford.

**Mitchell:** If you're around I could discuss that with you.

**Jack:** Probably you're going to need somebody else to help you with the rent. You have time to figure that out.

I talked to Richie Zorn, and he was wondering what you were doing. He knows you're doing very well and thought you were looking for a full-time job. He's on one of the boards for the new medical center.

They have a large administrative office. Richie was wondering if you might be interested in working in the business end of the medical center. They're looking for people to fit into the organization. They want to hire community people, if they're responsible enough.

**Mitchell:** That's a good possibility.

**Jack:** Do you want me to do some research about that?

**Mitchell:** That would be fine.

**Barbara:** If Dad's going to do some research with the Hudson Valley Medical Center and other possible jobs, you're going to have to get some things in place. What will you need to put in place?

**Mitchell:** I need to put together a résumé and a letter of application. And references, which I definitely have.

**Barbara:** You start working on your part of it, with a résumé. Dad will start working on maybe setting up some interviews.

**Mitchell:** When are we going to start things?

**Jack:** In the spring.

**Mitchell:** Okay.

**Jack:** If we think about late spring. Next time we're together, we'll put together a timetable. The summer would be nice.

We're very proud of how well you've done at Jespy. You've done a lot there. You couldn't do this if you hadn't done that. They taught you a lot of things. We're really very proud of you.

**Mitchell:** Yeah.

*May '93*

**Jason:** We have a problem here. The way I feel about college, the plan is, in my perception, that I have to keep right on going to my high school junior and my senior year and then go to college. I want to accomplish that the skills that I have learned from my senior year in high school—half work and half independence and half academics—I'm going to make even better by going to college.

After I go to college . . . I would now be fully independent and do work in the community with a high-paying job to support myself with my wife and make history with her. . . . That's what my goal is . . . to have history with my future wife.

Let's think about the tortoise and the hare. I am the tortoise because I do things slow and I get much better when I'm slow. Even though I have pain to do it, but you can accomplish anything. . . . You'll get much better and you'll learn a lot when you are slow like the tortoise. One step at a time.

The hare rushed through and starts to feel tired and I can

make the translation on the tortoise and the hare. Mitchell is the hare because he is rushing through. In my opinion...I don't think he should skip college. There's lots of things he might learn because at college prepares him for his future.

He does not go anywhere if he skips college. He goes into an apartment with his friends to prepare him for the future. What I'm saying is that there is a big gap right before Jespy and his senior year of high school.... I advise him that he should go back to college.

**Emily:** Well, he did almost two years at Jespy and now he's going to move into his own place and he's starting a good job at the Peekskill/Cortlandt Chamber of Commerce. He'll be working as an office assistant, answering phones, helping to give out information to walk-in customers, filing, faxing, and working on database computer projects. So he seems to be doing okay.

**Jason:** What I'm saying is, he's getting his low-paying job at the Chamber of Commerce. To make a high-paying job is get the skills what you need at college right before Jespy so he would have more feedback to his future.

I'm really worried about Mitchell's future and his success because he doesn't go anywhere and it doesn't make sense that he skips college. I think he jumped the gun. I am going to take it easy and slow. Maybe he can still take courses in college to prepare him for his future. College is important plus independence and work. Both of us want to have good high-paying jobs and a good future. I wish the best for him and I wish for him to have a good life because he is really my friend. I respect a lot about him. And I care for him.

**Emily:** Guess what I just found out? Westchester Community College will be opening a new northern campus just one block from where Mitchell's job will be. I hear that he's planning to take some college courses there.

**Jason:** I think that's wonderful.... Now he's learning that the college is very important to him. I'm so glad that he's [going to be] taking some college courses. That will make a good difference in his life, and I hope he'll never skip college any more. I've been taking so slow to move up to my future and I wish that he would do [that], too. I think it will be a better future for him. It will sharpen his skills for what he needs to be an independent person. That's what college is.

*January '93*

**Mitchell:** We should reflect on one important issue which I feel is important: What you plan on doing for the rest of your life. That's important. That's what people really want to know when they read this book. What are our plans, to be exact.

**Jason:** My definition of life is: A Learning Adventure. You have to learn a lot of good stuff. You have to accept the fact that it might be dangerous. It's all part of your abilities.

**Mitchell:** The important thing is about addressing all of the issues. I'm not talking about politics. I'm talking in general. I'm talking about you and me. What abilities that we can do and what we cannot do.

This should be a very interesting year from my perspective. There are many things we're looking forward to. One of the important key issues, not to be too political, is how are we going to support ourselves? Financially and otherwise. I know our parents have supported us throughout our whole entire life. Now I'm curious, what will happen with the rest of our life. I know we have the support from them, but how are we going to do that on our own independently? It takes a lot of abilities and skills and both me and Jason need to work on that a lot more.

**Jason:** The other thing about accepting what life is, is to know your goals. So you can remember and study them hard so you can learn more deeply and move on through your life. What they are and deciding if they are real or not real.

**Mitchell:** People are not perfect. People make mistakes.

**Jason:** Well, you can learn from that, too.

**Mitchell:** One of the things about life... and what you said about having a goal, certain things need to be put into perspective. To me, for my observation, it is important for everyone to realize that we need to have our minds open... that any opportunity can come at any given time. If we don't have it open, how can we succeed in life?

**Jason:** Do the things that you *can* do... and learn the things that you *can't* do. When you learn the things that you *can't* do, it then becomes the things you *can* do.

# Afterword

**Barbara and Emily:** Throughout Mitchell and Jason's early years, we were told to anticipate that their development would slow down, plateau, and eventually stop. On the contrary, we have observed that, like everyone else, people with Down syndrome continue to grow and learn throughout their lifetime, and to benefit from new opportunities and experiences.

People often ask us what we anticipate for Mitchell and Jason further down the road. Will they marry? Will they drive? Will they live on their own? Will they be self-reliant?

The answer is that we're not sure about any of these things. However, we have learned over the years not to have limited expectations for our sons. We wish for them the same things we wish for our other children: good health; a sense of satisfaction in their work; caring family and friends; and, possibly, the security, companionship, and fulfillment of an enduring love relationship.

We hope they will continue to have a close and meaningful relationship with each other — one that will grow over the years and will always be an important part of their lives.

It is apparent to us that Mitchell and Jason understand the special challenges they face, but this understanding does not diminish their capacity to enjoy life to the fullest. They are looking forward with excitement to the many new adventures yet to come.

This book is ending, but new chapters are writing themselves every day.

# Acknowledgments

We would like to express our deep gratitude to Rubin Pfeffer, President of the Trade Division at Harcourt Brace & Company, for his belief in the value and merit of this project and the importance of its message.

Our special thanks to Ruth Greenstein, our editor, for her constant commitment to maintaining the honesty and integrity of the manuscript and her sensitivity, encouragement, and support of Mitchell and Jason in seeing this book come to fruition.

**—E.P.K. and B.G.L.**

>>$9.95
(HIGHER IN CANADA)

Family/Special Education/Psychology

"A celebration of triumph over expectations."　　　—*Kirkus Reviews*

In this ground-breaking volume, Mitchell Levitz (22) and Jason Kingsley (19) share their innermost thoughts, feelings, hopes and dreams, their lifelong friendship—and their experiences of growing up with Down syndrome.

*Count Us In* draws from more than fifty conversations Mitchell and Jason had over the course of three years. With wit, intelligence, candor, and charm, these two young men speak about what matters most in their lives: careers, friendships, school, sex, marriage, politics, finances, and independence. While their concerns echo those of most young people at the cusp of adulthood, they also reflect the special challenges of growing up with a disability.

In telling us about themselves *in their own words,* Mitchell and Jason make a powerful and inspirational statement about the full potential of people with developmental disabilities.

"This single volume will do more to change stereotypes about Down syndrome than any book I have ever read."

　　　　　—Mary L. Coleman, M.D., Emeritus, Georgetown University

"Jason and Mitchell talk openly to one another and to others, and out of these discussions come messages about people with Down syndrome that the whole world needs to hear."

　　　　　—Robert Perske, author of *Circles of Friends*

**Mitchell Levitz** graduated from high school in 1991. He is active in politics, has worked for two state assembly members, and presently lives and works in Peekskill, New York. **Jason Kingsley** is a high school senior and former associate board member of the National Down Syndrome Congress. He has acted in films and on television and currently lives in Chappaqua, New York.

A portion of the authors' royalties from this book will be donated to the National Down Syndrome Congress and the National Down Syndrome Society.

Cover photo by Richard Hutchings

A Harvest Original
Harcourt Brace & Company
*525 B Street, San Diego, CA 92101*
*15 East 26th Street, New York, NY 10010*

ISBN 0-15-622660-X

90000>

9 780156 226608